Editorial

D'aithle na bhfileadh n-uasal,
  truaghsan timheal an tsaoghail;
clann na n-ollamhgo n-eagna
  folamh gan freagra faobhair...

The high poets are gone
  and I mourn for the world's waning,
the sons of those learned masters
  emptied of sharp response.

In April 2020 we lost Eavan Boland and in December 2021 Thomas Kinsella. I say 'we' selfishly, because *PN Review* is in part their construction and became their magazine for decades. Eavan was first reviewed in *PNR* 2 and contributed major poems, essays, reviews and interviews from 1985 ('Listen. This is the Noise of Myth' was the first). Tom was first mentioned in *Poetry Nation II* by Donald Davie in his famous essay 'The Varsity Match', and started contributing in person in 1993. In 2015 and 2016 we published his 'personal readings' of Dickinson, Yeats, Beckett and Wordsworth.

Observing these great Irish poets through the lens of the magazine, over a long period when they were in uncertain motion in time and in the world, finding their divergent ways, they are tentative, alive, working their ways towards the completion of their books and projects but not yet, not quite there, as in those wonderfully re-defining interviews they give, candid and generous. For them what begins as a 'dual tradition' develops in complexity, more strands add themselves; as time passes the always problematic and often vexing fact of Great Britain dwindles in importance. To *PN Review* this was an enabling process, too: based in Manchester, it too found centres beyond the main English publishing centre in which earlier Anglophone writers – Irish, American, Caribbean, Indian – had come for validation.

Thomas Kinsella became a resister of the literary energies that emanated from Oxbridge and the commercial interests of London publishing. When I first came to Britain in 1965, he was the main up-and-coming Irish poet of the day, his collections published by Oxford University Press, a familiar of the Movement poets and closely associated with Donald Davie in Dublin. Eavan Boland remembered how, 'By the time I went to Trinity in the early 1960s I could feel the change. Irish poetry was beginning to report something new. It came down to simple things. The inclusion of the city was one of them -- the sights and sounds and streets. Looking at Kinsella's "Another September" and "Downstream" you can see where those city images are going: into a harsh, interesting dialogue with the Yeatsian pastoral. And it was worked through those urban images. Poems like "Baggot Street Deserta" were fresh and jagged.' (*PNR* 133, in the year 2000: the issue includes three poems by Kinsella.)

The city was not a generic city, it was Dublin; its jaggedness was evidence of a specific history. Writing a note to accompany the poems we published in the 100th issue of *PNR*, *A Calendar of Modern Poetry*, in 1994, Kinsella said,

My first poems were written partly in curiosity, with my discovery of modern poetry. And in some excitement, with the discovery of my own personal world

– in detail – in *Dubliners* and *A Portrait of the Artist as a Young Man.*

It was a while before my poems could say exactly what I wanted them to say. As I began to manage this, I wrote a number of poems out of a strong local sense, with an awareness of things against their routine backgrounds. 'Chrysalides' and 'Westland Row' are two of these. Later, I found reality and the past expressing themselves in a sense of family, in memories of my growing up in Dublin. In my attempts at generalisation, and making sense of experience that mattered, I wrote mainly longer poems; but 'Artists' Letters' and 'Talent and Friendship' are shorter poems of this kind.

When I try to write about these ideas, I find that I am more at ease in poetry. 'At the Head Table' is a recent long poem; the first part has to do with possible attitudes of the artist toward his work and toward his audience.

His resistance to the conventional centre cost him the central reputation he had when I first encountered his work. Davie remembers (*Poetry Nation II*, 1974) how when Larkin was trying to find a publisher for *The Less Deceived* he looked to Ireland: 'it is worth putting it on record that a version of that collection had earlier been rejected, by the Dolmen Press in Dublin. (The Irishmen who turned it down, Liam Miller, Sean White, Tom Kinsella, rejected Larkin for the same reason presumably as the Scotsman Tom Scott rejects him now... Larkin's English admirers do not recognise how non-exportable he is, even within the British Isles.)' Eloquent parentheses. It is not that Kinsella recoiled from Larkin's work – he could speak of it with appreciation. But in publishing terms it did not belong in Ireland.

At first, Kinsella was identified with the Movement poets, but soon – despite his remarkable formal resources and his ironies – his differences became apparent. In particular, his kinds of irony, fraught with anger, were different from his English contemporaries'. In *PN Review 1* the American critic Calvin Bedient wrote an essay on what he dubbed 'Absentist poetry' and placed the Irish poet in the formal and thematic company of W.S. Graham, Geoffrey Hill and Ted Hughes.

In the introduction to his *New Oxford Book of Irish Verse* (1987) he puts more distance between himself and the British fashions of the day. He resisted the idea of an Ulster Renaissance, omitting Michael Longley, Tom Paulin, Paul Muldoon and others from the book. Further, he insisted on the specifically Irish strand: 'the Irish tradition is a matter of two linguistic entities in dynamic interaction, of two major bodies of poetry asking to be understood together as functions of a shared and painful history' – Irish providing 'the oldest vernacular literature in Western Europe'. The relationship between these two strands at different periods in Irish history illuminates the cultural dynamic. Kinsella's work as a translator is part of the magnificence of his achievement. He attended an Irish-language school and the language was deeply rooted in him.

Even in the early 1970s, some English critics began to say that Kinsella had taken a 'wrong turn', i.e., he had turned *away*, in his critical writing and in poems like 'Nightwalker', 'Phoenix Park', 'Downstream' and in his controversial, immediate response to Bloody Sunday in 1972, *Butcher's Dozen*, re-published by Carcanet as Peppercanister 30 to mark the fiftieth anniversary of the events. His hectic revision of his poems was part of this struggle away, freeing himself from association with his British contemporaries. Other more amenable Irish poets were soon taken up. He retained his American and Irish readers, and became an increasingly radical poetic and therefore political presence. His Peppercanister Press was a route to independence – an independence which almost courted neglect. Reviewing his *Selected Poems* in these pages in 2008 my co-editor John McAuliffe wrote, 'Other contributing factors to his low profile reflect a literary culture increasingly focused on festivals and prize shortlists for single collections,' trends amply chronicled in our pages.

His irreplaceable translation of *The Táin* is a permanent addition to the Irish canon, through which elements of the dual tradition will survive. The creative and linguistic work on *The Táin* complicated his English poetry and led into his challenging, mature work, in particular *New Poems 1973*. In McAuliffe's words, 'readers will get a good sense of the poems' plumbing of idiomatic "spoken" English, and their astonishing, perspective-switching movement between the myths of early Irish settlement and Kinsella's own childhood and adult life, and, framing all this effort, a Beckett-like vision which might be summed up by Pozzo's "giving birth

astride a grave, the light gleams an instant then it's night once more".' And McAu-
liffe quotes, as I shall to close, lines from 'At the Head Table' (1991), 'whose speaker
is modelled on Swift and Aogán Ó Rathaille':

> The air grew dark with anger
> toward the close of the celebration.
> But remembering his purpose
> he kept an even temper
>
> thinking: I have devoted
> my life, my entire career,
> to the avoidance of affectation,
> the way of entertainment
>
> or the specialist response.
> With always the same outcome.
> Dislike. Misunderstanding.
> But I will do what I can.

Letter to the Editor

Walter Bruno writes A response to Charlie Louth's invig-
orating take (*PNR* 262, p. 38) on Mahon's translation of
'The Gypsies' (a traditional spelling I tend to use). The
Mahon translation is fairly broad, broader than Louth
suggests. 'La nation' in continental French is the French
nation itself, not 'nations' as the translation posits. It's
'the people'. This is clearly to demark the non-French
Roma from their hosts; which makes it harder to agree
with Louth's assertion, that Gypsies are 'not the subject'
of the poem, notwithstanding the transferences which
Louth very adroitly discusses. Still, an open fire is the
eternal sign of hunter-forager 'encampment' and Paris
settlement is the classical rebuke of that, a place of fire
prohibitions; and that seems essential. Indeed, this
poem is almost entirely about transience, versus a cur-
fewed and settled town. The 'fear' expressed in the
poem's end is the fear of Roma extinctions, and the
'light' is metaphor for their endurance.

It's useful to note that, too, that reference to Robinson
in 'La Voix', removed by Mahon, is targeted and precise.
Robinson is a terminal rail point, and a suburban sign
in Parisian parlance. Finally, here's my own ad-hoc trans-
lation of Les Gitans:

> There is a fire under the trees;
> we hear it speak low
> to the sleeping people,
> we, near the gates.
> If we go silently, we
> short-lived souls,
> between the shrouded flats,
> it is only in fear that you
> die out, you eternal
> crackle of hidden light.

His hair was the razor wire that patrolled Victorian
  walls
And his mouth a hidden tunnel burrowed beneath
  concrete.
But his heart. His heart.
His heart was a home. Lamp lit. Early dusk. As the
Children walk clumsily home from school.
  (from 'Home is Where the Heart is')

On 11 January the 2021 T.S. Eliot prize was awarded to **Joelle Taylor** for *C+nto & Othered Poems* (Westbourne Press), described by Glyn Maxwell, chair of the judges, as 'a blazing book of rage and light, a grand opera of liberation from the shadows of indifference and oppression.' This is her fourth collection. She is a generous and an enabling activist, running workshops where they might matter (as at Wandsworth Prison), promoting the work of others. At the Southbank she hosts the London-based night of poetry and music, Out-Spoken. She has published plays and short stories as well.

*

The 2021 Queen's Gold Medal for Poetry was awarded to **Grace Nichols**, in particular for her first book of poems *I Is a Long-Memoried Woman* (which won the Commonwealth Poetry Prize in 1983), her prose, and several books for younger readers. 'Over the past four decades,' the poet laureate Simon Armitage declared, 'Grace has been an original, pioneering voice in the British poetry scene. Her poems are alive with characters from the folklore and fables of her Caribbean homeland, and echo with the rhymes and rhythms of her family and ancestors... They are also passionate and sensuous at times, being daring in their choice of subject and openhearted in their outlook. Above all, Grace Nichols has been a beacon for black women poets in this country, staying true to her linguistic coordinates and poetic sensibilities, and offering a means of expression that has offered inspiration and encouragement to many.' Her husband John Agard was awarded the Medal in 2012, the first time a single household has boasted two. 'In my own work,' she said, 'I've celebrated my Guyanese/Caribbean/South American heritage in relation to the English traditions we inherited as a former British colony. To poetry and the English language that I love, I've brought the registers of my own Caribbean tongue. I wish my parents who used to chide me for straining my eyes, as a small girl reading by torchlight in bed, were around to share in this journey that poetry has blessed me with.'

*

Portuguese poet **Ana Luísa Amaral** received the 2021 Queen Sofía Award for Iberoamerican Poetry on 7 November. The award was conferred at the University of Salamanca. She is the thirtieth recipient. The award recognises the entirety of the poet's work and its literary value to the cultural patrimony of Iberoamerica and Spain. Amaral was born in 1956 in Lisbon. She is one of the most celebrated Portuguese writers of recent times. A professor at the University of Porto, she took her doctorate in the poetry of Emily Dickinson and has published widely on Anglophone poetry, comparative literature and feminist studies. The award entails a generous sum of cash and a scholarly, annotated edition of some of the writer's work.

The occasion also presented an opportunity to remember and celebrate those previous award winners who had recently died, among them major figures including Caballero Bonald, Francisco Brines, Ernesto Cardenal and Joan Margarit.

*

John Lucas writes: The death has occurred of **Tim Thorne**, Australian poet, publisher, and important promoter of poetry in Tasmania. Born in 1944, Thorne spent most of his life in his native state, although during the late 1960s he lived in Sydney, where he was closely associated with *Poetry Magazine* (later *New Poetry),* and startled the natives by appearing in public in a long cloak and beret. This was deliberately intended as a show of homage to nineteenth Century French poets at a time when other poets connected to Sydney were busy rejecting the influence of English poetry in favour of, among others, Mallarmé and Rimbaud, though Thorne's familiarity with the French language provided a large measure of authenticity for his avowed admiration of Baudelaire.

Back in Tasmania, and by now married to his life-long love and companion, Stephanie, Thorne settled in Launceston, from where he began the wonderfully lively Tasmanian Poetry Festivals, of which he was director for seventeen years, and to which, with some financial assistance from the Australian Arts Council, he invited a large number of internationally-known poets, as well as important Tasmanian writers, including such luminaries as Gwen Harwood, Andrew Sant, Margaret Scott, and Vivian Smith. During these years he founded The Cornford Press, under which imprint he published pamphlets and whole collections of work by a variety of young or hitherto little-known poets. A man of outstanding energy and generosity, Thorne's reputation as a poet was secured by the publication, in 2008, of *I Con: New and Selected Poems*, published by Salt in both Australia and the UK. That came after the publication of at least a dozen individual collections and would be followed by others. His work is represented in the UK by *The Bloodaxe Book of Modern Australian Poetry,* 1994), first published in Australia in 1991 as *The Penguin Book of Modern Australian Poetry.*

A principled socialist, Thorne never used poetry as a means of preaching to the converted, is often sharply satirical; and his formal adroitness – he was especially resourceful in his use of rhyme and half-rhyme – makes his best work memorably sharp-edged. 'Sight Screen' is the punning title for a poem about the defection of one-time Australian cricket captain Kim Hughes to play in apartheid South Africa after he had burst into tears (blinded by them) on a tour of England when matters were going badly against the old enemy. 'Blindness is only a virtue in justice,' Thorne writes, 'or else black and white look unalike/and a keen eye can pick out/a lethal delivery against a coloured crowd.' This was written at a time when Tasmania was becoming increasingly troubled over the treatment by nineteenth-century settlers of the island's original population, but its relevance extends beyond any particular moment or place.

*

Raúl Rivero, the Cuban journalist, poet and eventually a radical opponent of the Castro regime, imprisoned for subversion due to his insistence on an independent press in his country, died in Florida on 6 November. He was 75 years old.

He had been a chief correspondent in Moscow for the Cuban news agency for three years, from 1973, then a culture editor for Union of Writers and Artists of Cuba publications. He initially hailed Castro in these terms: 'the dreams of human redemption sung by the bearded victors of 1959' and was regarded as the revolution's poet. But he went beyond his ideological remit, especially after the collapse of the Soviet Union in 1989. He and other Cuban intellectuals petitioned the authorities to increase civil liberties, hold elections and free political prisoners. Journalism should no longer uphold the 'fiction about a country that does not exist'. His efforts became known and celebrated abroad, he was singled out by Reporters Without Borders in 1997 and received the Maria Moors Cabot Prize from Columbia University

in 1999. In 2000, the International Press Institute named him one of the world's 50 heroes of press freedom.

He and others established the Association of Cuban Journalists in 2001. They published two issues of *De Cuba* magazine before Castro's 'Black Spring' that rejected the petition. Many arrests were made, Rivero among them. He was charged as a 'paid collaborator with a hostile country' – the northern neighbour – and sentenced to twenty years in prison. He wrote his collection *Life and Offices* (published in 2006) from his cramped cell. His confinement in the end lasted a year, then he was released with others in a gesture of appeasement to the EU. In 2004, he was awarded the Guillermo Cano World Press Freedom Prize for his life's work by UNESCO.

*

The American writer best known for his poetry **David Wagoner** died on 18 December at the age of 95. His main fame was in the Pacific Northwest of the United States, his poems (more than twenty volumes over a long lifetime) informed by his childhood there and by the vivid geography and climate. In 1991 he won the Ruth Lilly Poetry Prize. One of the prize judges, Rita Dove, declared, 'He has never imitated himself. He has always moved in deeper directions; he has always been exploring something new.' He was a precursor to the eco-poetry movement, a conservationist.

No two trees are the same to Raven.
No two branches are the same to Wren.
If what a tree or a bush does is lost on you,
You are surely lost. Stand still. The forest knows
Where you are. You must let it find you.

At Theodore Roethke's suggestion the University of Washington hired Wagoner in 1954 and 48 years later he retired as poet emeritus. He edited *Poetry Northwest* from 1966 to 2002, introducing and honouring numerous poets in its pages.

*

Michael Schmidt writes: When *Poetry Nation* began, **Robert Bly**'s name was much in currency. In the first issue James Atlas commented on the Minnesota poet's translation work, Robert Shaw on his debts to Ginsberg. He referred to *The Teeth-Mother Naked At Last* as 'a sort of up-dated, outward-looking *Howl*', The concern with violence and racism at the time of Vietnam and the protest movement was vividly evoked, but also with a touch of the academy in its strategies: 'In an apocalyptic patch Bly envisages the nation as finally polarised, young set against old, the peace movement against the increasingly authoritarian government (the "teeth-mother")' and he quotes:

Now the whole nation starts to whirl,
the end of the Republic breaks off,
Europe comes to take revenge,
the mad beast covered with European hair rushes
    through the mesa bushes

in Mendochino County,
pigs rush toward the cliff,
    the waters underneath part, in one ocean lumi-
    nous globes float up (in them
hairy and ecstatic rock musicians) –
in the other, the teeth-mother, naked at last.

Bly makes an appearance even in the editorial which laments his and Denise Levertov's turn to vehement protest poetry. In *Poetry Nation* 2 Jeffrey Wainwright quotes from his interview with Neruda: he was at the centre of our sense of the contemporary, and not just contemporary American poetry. He branded *For the Union Dead* a counterfeit and seemed bound – with his comrades – in quite another direction. As time passed, he became less important to *PNR* contributors and readers, referred to as a major translator of contemporary poetry and, in a brilliant essay by Eavan Boland, described as a quondam pastoral poet who had proceeded to 'the violated pastoral -- whether regional or global' which is 'all that's left of that landscape. But this is not new. The poem of disappointed expectations, of spoiled hopes remains a cultural seismograph today as it did in earlier times. The site where a deeply private experience of loss, illness, estrangement puts a proper stress on language remains a rich source. Above all, form and its likely fragmentation in the face of intense experience is a central theme.'

His most widely read work was and perhaps still is *Iron John: a Book About Men* (1990), arguing against the sissi-fication of American man, and advocating the restoration of what the *New York Times* called 'primal male audacity [...] He held men-only seminars and weekend retreats, gatherings often in the woods with men around campfires thumping drums, making masks, hugging, dancing and reading poetry aloud.' It seemed to some a harsh response to feminism, to others a parody or comedy: 'Cartoonists and talk-show hosts ridiculed it, dismissing it as tree-hugging self-indulgence by middle-class baby boomers.'

Bly, a year junior to Wagoner, died a few days after him, at 94. His passing marks the end of an extraordinary publishing phenomenon, with a library of over 50 books of poetry and translation to his credit, and an enormous investment in the advocacy and translation of major Latin American and European writers.

For my generation the poet of snowy fields and rural quiet became the strident voice of public protest, just as we were coming of age and the Vietnam War was hotting up and threatening to include us. His poems named names: President Johnson, Defense Secretary McNamara, Dean Rusk, General Westmoreland... He co-founded American Writers Against the Vietnam War. The reading tours and protests he organised were in a sense the crucible for the public poetry that has followed in the States and around the Anglophone world. He became quieter in later years but the fires he lighted are still burning.

Reports

Sitting with Discomfort

Part 1: What Kind of Room Is a Stanza?

VAHNI CAPILDEO

The kind of things that might be kept behind glass glisten, not even out on display, simply and perilously out for everyday use, despite and because of their breakability, in certain kinds of room. I mean such things as hand-embroidered cloths, high-quality china, and embellished glass, not weapons (or not so much). For some reason, those rooms are dimly lit. Like snowscapes, the faces of people catch whatever dusty light they can, never mind whether the people are dark-skinned or paler. Their human expressions appear partial and heightened, often with a doll-like anguish.

Poets like Natalie Linh Bolderston, Amy Key, and Sharon Olds are inheritors of such atmospheres. They do not need to tell stories to deal with interiority in ways that novelists traditionally have done, even though they often choose to recount situations or imply a narrative. The online journal *Peony Moon*, covering Amy Key's *Luxe* (Salt, 2013), reproduces poems such as 'To a Clothes Rail', which concludes:

Formal wear gown for selling on eBay
Dress bought for funeral, frequently worn to detach
    from death
Dress last worn when someone cried for you
Fretful dress, to be cut up for rags
Palladium dress for looking into mirrors in
A cake of a dress – whipped to frou-frou
Scented dress of mustard seed, orange peel and
    almond milk
Glitter-bellied hummingbird dress
Ex-favourite dress, now not quite right
Perfectly acceptable dress, given the circumstances

The dressed body is a thing of circumstance, nightmare and dream. The poet's list is like an exercise in how to inhabit 'self' plausibly; is it for flying, for mourning, for being decorative or edible? It laughs at its own inability to come to rest. Some of these dresses might as well figure in Agatha Christie as in Plath; in M.R.

James as in Marianne Moore. Natalie Linh Bolderston, whose poem 'Middle Name with Diacritics' was shortlisted for in the Forward Prizes Best Single Poem category (2021), creates a four-part sequence unpacking the meanings of that name, through shades of 'soul', 'soldier', 'bravery' and 'to command'. The meanings do not arrive as definitions. So much more than a gold, silver, or rainbow evening dress unfolding from a nutshell in a fairytale, entire landscapes and eras unfold from the name. The first part of the sequence opens:

Lính [soldier]

1. Two sisters / who delivered a village from the
    throat / of a tiger / the
    Red River's champions / anointed as queens
2. A woman / their descendant / two hundred years
    later / who carried
    girls from the betrayal of moonlight / searched a
    field / for the skinless face / of
    someone she loved

So much more than a gold, silver, or rainbow evening dress unfolding from a nutshell in a fairytale, entire landscapes and eras unfold from the name. The name is story and history, enough for an epic. Instead, it is something by which the poet is known in life off the page, but only in a simplified version. The extra-textual has the thinness of ghost. The text has the life of the word.

Interiors, with their wealth of enforced roles and inescapable mirrors, are what people might have aspired to, or taken for granted, in late nineteenth-century and early twentieth-century Britain; in New England, too, perhaps; and interiors like that continue to exist in the former colonies, blooming with the layered ghosts of the global south. Old ladies' faces have been reflected in the dark shine of mahogany cupboard doors. Teacups expect to be placed in saucers. Perfume has decayed into the lining of chests of drawers. The legs of the piano teacher's husband, abruptly dead, stick out from amongst the legs of the furniture behind the French doors of the front parlour, visible to the teenaged music students waiting, shocked yet demure, in the wooden porch with its view of a double flower border, and its depressed dog, well-behaved and plagued by ticks. When you read Vivek Narayanan, Lorna Goodison, or Nicholas Laughlin, rooms like this haunt at least some of the stanzas, even if not evoked or itemized.

The 1993 film of Edith Wharton's 1920 novel, *The Age of Innocence*, was bound to disappoint, I thought. It failed to disappoint. It offers another series of insights and evocations into the uncanniness of inherited conventions and their transgression, the uncanniness of dwelling among handcrafted objects and the unfree circulation of imperial loot. The focus moves between fragile material things and emotionally pent-up human beings. The viewer feels appropriately trapped. I had been afraid there would be gross close-ups of actors with free-and-easy body language betraying the claustrophobia of the story they were meant to portray and jarring with their historical dress.

Fortunately, this was not the case. Instead, the camerawork tricked the viewer's eye and imagination from one beautiful, frustrating preoccupation or irrelevance into another. This produced the same feeling as the irritating, hypnotic intricacies of the novelist's syntax, when the silent reader tries to imagine a world from the words on the page. The interiors (in both senses) were recognizable: overfurnished rooms constraining bodies that must move in certain ways and usually must not touch; rooms scented with hot emotion, too airless for that emotion's expression. I wonder whether poets changing under the pressure of the coronavirus pandemic will begin to produce room-haunted stanzas again, furnishing text with the emotions of people who must not touch except in ritualized or dangerous ways.

In the old texts from the also-but-differently bad old days long before the plague, you can revel in the suggestion that what was unsaid was unsayable. It is as if the codes of politeness, the understatements, exclamations,

and broken-off sentences, are flat only like the flat surface of a sea which might trick a swimmer into calm places interlaced with fatal currents and unexpected drops of sea floor level from standing height to coldest depth. When the characters do very little and say not much, you may be sure that all sorts of passions are in play, all sorts of analyses taking place, secretly, in between the lines. Semicolons, ellipses, and dashes seem like the vital signs of the body of the text, a text of great heart and accelerated breathing. You are tossed about by its subconscious; you are not given that subconscious turned inside out.

It follows, from these reticences and failures, that in poems or novels too easily dismissed as baffling or ornamented, any level of event or plot twist may be shocking, but not wholly surprising, because they are profoundly truthful to human extremes. Whether a character runs away with a lover, or commits murder, or incarcerates themself in respectability forever, the unspeakable and the spoken remain wrapped around each other, like clingfilm and seaweed around today's unfortunate sea-creatures. May Emily Dickinson's teasing of eternity through brevity overpower Walt Whitman's long rumbles? Certainly, the basic violence of Jane Austen's blithe and transparent telling, in which enslavement, abduction, injury and war are seldom more than a trip away, is tougher than Charlotte Brontë's. The mud, glitter, and rape that growl and hallelujah through Shivanee Ramlochan are no more or less intense than the scalpel-like processes of Sophie Collins.

How is it possible to read all these texts in a way that meets them where they are? What is a reader to do?

This is the first part of a two-part essay. The second part will look at the speakable and the unspeakable in the context of 'sitting with discomfort', via close reading of Solmaz Sharif and Dionne Brand. While the first part has kept circling back to exteriors, things, places, and embodiment in their relation to text, the second part, will deal acutely with blanks and gaps in specific poetic texts, and offer techniques for a practice of reading that refuses to edit out the reader's own bodily cues.

Last Thoughts on Thirty-Five Years of Poems on the Underground

JUDITH CHERNAIK

Poems on the Underground went live on London's tube cars in 1986 – which means that we reached our thirty-fifth year in 2021. But what an age away it seems, with London barely recovering from lockdown, borders to Europe and the rest of the world in chaos, pundits and politicians alike baffled by the new reality. The folly of Brexit seems a minor hiccup in the larger global catastrophe.

Still, poetry survives, a witness to times past and present. It is a quiet pleasure to know that we've contributed to its wider circulation. The project has changed with

the years. Gerard Benson died in 2014, and Cicely has stepped back. I've been joined as co-editors by Imtiaz Dharker and George Szirtes, who have added their own special passions to our choice of poems. We continue to enjoy the support of London Underground, as well as the general public, and, above all, the poets featured on the tube.

When we were paused on the tube, in the first London lockdown, we set up a website (www.poemsontheunderground.org) featuring our original posters in digitised form, with poems added each month. Over a year later, the website is turning into an archive of all our posters from the first set onward, reaching eventually a total of more than 600 poems.

As I'm cast back to our beginnings, I feel quite nostalgic about the origin of a simple project which has reached world fame. I was young then, in my 40s, as were my friends Gerard and Cicely. I was in love with London, with all its faults, a city in which novels by Dickens and Trollope were visible on the streets, in bodies curled in doorways, in second-hand bookshops and jumble sales. Not only Victorian novelists but the poets I loved, Milton, Blake, Shelley and many others, raged against conditions which had hardly changed, or so it seemed to me.

I am often asked if there was any wider purpose inspiring the project. Not really – it was more a natural extension of friendship, shared discoveries. Gerard and Cicely were trained actors and speakers of verse. They were members of the Barrow Poets – four readers and two musicians – equally at home performing in primary schools and pubs, at intimate theatre spaces and in the Queen Elizabeth Hall, sold out each Christmas for a week of their children's concerts. We were friends and neighbours, and when Gerard started an informal play-reading group, meeting once a month, my husband and I were invited along. At a reading of *As You Like It*, with Cicely playing Rosalind, I was charmed by the lovesick Orlando, read by Gerard, posting amateurish love sonnets on trees in the Forest of Arden. It was a short step to the idea of posting poems on the advertising spaces in London tube cars.

The morning after the play-reading, I wrote to 'The Manager, London Underground' asking whether poems might be used to fill empty advertising spaces. To my surprise, I had a response within days, expressing interest, and referring me to the Advertising Manager, a Mr Joe Putnam. We met at his office in Camden Town, a short bus ride from my home. He proposed that if my friends and I could raise enough money to pay for some advertising spaces for poems, at £5 per space for two months, he would happily double the number. He suggested that we aim for about 500 spaces, thus £2500 – not an impossible sum.

How simple life was at that time! London Underground ran its own advertising, prices were reasonable, and Joe, it turned out, played the 'Dame' in Christmas pantomimes, enjoyed reading poetry, and was an altogether genial man. The Underground had a proud history of encouraging fine design in typography as well as architecture, and included lines by Shakespeare and Keats in its own early posters. We were just carrying on a tradition.

By chance, the New Statesman back page included a notice inviting applications to the Arts Council for a project 'to promote the wider reading of poetry.' I applied to the Betty Compton fund, set up for the purpose, for £3,000 to put poems on Tube trains, with an estimated potential readership in the millions. £2500 would pay for the spaces; £500 for design, printing and any extra expenses. Desmond Clarke, Marketing Director at Faber & Faber Publishers, was keen to carry on the legacy of their first Poetry Editor, T.S. Eliot. He offered to have Faber design and print the posters at no charge. As we waited for the Arts Council to consider our proposal, I had a confidential phone call from the writer Claire Tomalin, who told me that Philip Larkin, who was on the committee, feared that the project would be too left wing. Claire suggested that I write to him explaining that we had no political agenda. This was quite true, since Underground by-laws forbid the display on their property of any party-political material, or anything calculated to cause offence. We hoped to feature Milton, Blake and Shelley, of course, as well as Adrian Mitchell and other radical poets; it would be hard to find an ode to capitalism or the free market. But I wrote to Mr Larkin as directed.

We had a friendly exchange of letters, in which Larkin told me that he liked the project, which reminded him of the notice boards outside churches, which often featured Biblical words of wisdom or consolation. The grant was awarded, and we agreed a set of poems to start – the left wing poets Shelley and Robert Burns, the American populist William Carlos Williams, and two young poets who were later to become well known, the British/Guyanese poet Grace Nichols and the Irish poet Seamus Heaney. Press and TV turned up to the launch at Aldwych Station, on the Strand, used for films about the London Blitz, now permanently shut. Everyone loved the poems and also loved the project.

So it has remained, for the past 35 years. London, global financial centre, has suffered fire and flood; the world has changed almost beyond recognition. Poetry continues to flourish, perhaps more significantly in bad times than in good. In 2021, we marked the 200th anniversary of the death of London's beloved poet, John Keats, who hoped that his poems would be 'a balm and comfort' to suffering humanity. In 2022 we'll mark the 200th anniversary of the death of Shelley, who believed fervently that poetry could change the world. The works and ideas of young poets sit easily on the tube alongside the classics, apparently welcomed by a potential readership of four million daily travellers. We hope to carry on until the welcome wears out.

Farida Majid Boughey (1942–2021)

JAMES SUTHERLAND-SMITH

Poets, readers of poetry and habitués of London's thriving poetry scene in the 1970s could not fail to have noticed a slender, extraordinarily beautiful woman of South Asian appearance, usually dressed in one of her four hundred saris, although sometimes she wore slacks, a T-shirt or roll-neck pullover if an event was wholly informal, and carrying a shopping bag filled with slim volumes from her own publishing venture, the Salamander Imprint. In addition to her physical presence, Farida had a commanding manner which made her the centre of attention. Friends and admirers included Jacques Derrida and the Guinness family heir, Gareth Browne the creator of Cladagh Records and supporter of the Irish traditional music group, The Chieftains. A number of poets were close friends and confidants; Fleur Adcock, Jim Burns, Gavin Ewart, Ted Hughes, George Macbeth, W.S. Merwin, John Montague, Christopher Reid and Kit Wright.

Farida Majid was born on 27 July 1942 in Kolkata, to Jochna, the daughter of the poet Golam Mostofa, who was responsible for the first translations of the Quran into Bangla, a task that Farida was to resume in the final period of her life. It was under the guidance of her grandfather that Farida developed as a poet although after school she began to study chemistry. In the early 1960s she moved to New York as part of a United Nations exchange programme for students and began to study literature at New York University. By the late sixties her marriage to the American architect, Robert Boughey, had fallen apart and she moved to London where she was active in promoting the independence of Bangladesh from Pakistan and becoming part of London's society of the poem, to adapt a phrase of Jonathan Raban's.

She set up the Salamander Imprint, beginning with her pamphlet of translations of Bangla poets. She published five collections by English language poets including a notable coup in Kit Wright's first collection, the award winning The Bear Looked Over the Mountain.

Farida also held court at her flat in Cadogan Square once a month on Thursdays to a salon of artists and poets which included Adcock, Ewart, Macbeth and Andrew Waterman, the inventor of mind maps, Tony Buzan, the poets and publishers Ian Robinson and John Welch and the cultural wheeler dealer, George Wightman. Wine was drunk and poets read a new poem which was then discussed. The Thursday Evening Anthology appeared in 1977 with sketches of the contributors by the artist, Feliks Topolski. The anthology is worth reading for Fleur Adcock's brilliant, restrained poem, 'Injury'. Its occasion is the aftermath of a violent assault on a woman by her lover.

In 1979 Farida took one of her frequent trips out of the UK and returned with the promise of an editing job at Harper's Magazine. This she declared as her reason for entry at immigration and was promptly asked for her work permit. It was 1979 and the easy-going regime of the past had changed. Despite our best efforts and lobbying of the media, she was deported back to the United States, of which she was a citizen. Poetry in Britain lost much glamour and a tireless advocate.

In New York, Farida became a lecturer at Columbia University, eventually returning to Dhaka in Bangladesh where she was a respected member of the literary community, translated the Quran and advocated the peaceful humaneness of Islam.

When I knew her in London she could be a delightful companion. One had to prepare to go home with the milk after a night out and often the first act of play would be missed due to her elaborate toilette, always completed by the placing of a bindi of appropriate colour in the centre of her forehead with the head of a six-inch nail which she kept on her dressing table for the purpose. Despite her physical beauty Farida was unsure of her appearance as her sister had been accounted by her family as the true beauty due to a lighter skin. In the mid-1970s, I once took tea at the Ritz with Farida, Gareth Browne and the late Grey Gowrie, who died four days before her in September 2021. His lordship declared that he ought to spend more time with writers. Farida retorted that as he'd written one book of poetry, he'd be wasting a life if he didn't write another one. Another time she kept the staff of a Bangla restaurant in the Fulham Road in thrall by singing them verses of Tagore.

Leasowe

HELEN TOOKEY

Seventh of November 2020. New Brighton, on the Wirral peninsula. I'm standing on the breakwater, looking out to sea. The surface under my feet is an odd mixture of rocks covered with a thin layer of something like tar, greyish, wrinkled, as though what I'm standing on is the long curving spine of some creature, with thick grey skin like an elephant. Just ahead of me, the tar layer ends, and the rocks are green with algae. It's a definite boundary, a place to stop. The tide is high, so the lighthouse, maybe thirty yards further out, is surrounded by water, though it's hard to tell how deep it is.

The other three are behind me, standing on the beach in a rough triangle, a few yards apart. We're not exactly meeting, and not exactly not meeting. Unable to organise anything formally, because of the restrictions, Bryan and I had simply emailed a few people – the Lowry 'regulars' – and said that we would be by the plaque on the prom, should they want to be there too. Alan has come from Hoylake, and Chris has walked up from Egremont. It's nice to see them, to feel that we haven't allowed the year to go by without some kind of marker. Mary has texted to say that she'll be sending us a wave from the beach at Ainsdale, further up the coast on the Liverpool side; later she sends Bryan a photo of the Day of the Dead tribute she's constructed on the sand, a Mexican carnival mask held down with seaweed and driftwood, a stick poking rather grimly through its eye-socket.

We take photographs of ourselves by the plaque, which sits like a blue porthole in the concrete sea-wall. *MALCOLM LOWRY / 1909–1957 / Author of Under the Volcano. Born in New Brighton*, the white text announces, with the quotation we had chosen: *The smoke of freighters outward bound from Liverpool hung low on the horizon.* Alan and I hold up our identical editions of *Under the Volcano*; with our masks and hats and dark glasses, we look like mountaineers or polar explorers, squinting into the sun, smiling for the camera. Then we walk on the beach, exchanging stories about the strangeness of the year, watching the container ships, which seem hardly to move and yet at the same time somehow to move extraordinarily fast, one minute at the river mouth, the next disappearing into the horizon. I leave the three of them chatting on the beach and walk out on the breakwater, which runs straight for a while and then curves leftwards, westward, away from the river. The lighthouse watches with a certain hauteur – it seems to scorn the notion of its own obsolescence, to have no truck with the fact that it was decommissioned nearly fifty years ago. It's easy to imagine this particular lighthouse as the one that Elizabeth Bishop describes in 'Seascape', 'standing there / in black and white clerical dress', the one who 'lives on his nerves, thinks he knows better'.

Alan and Chris go their separate ways and Bryan and I decide to walk along the seafront to Leasowe. It's early afternoon but seems later, a consequence maybe of the lack of definition to the day. The tide is still high enough to be lapping at the foot of the revetment, the long concrete slope that forms the sea defence along this stretch of coast. As always seems to be the case here, the sea is flat calm, it simply swells up against the concrete, only the tiniest suggestion of a wave in the backwash, and for ten or twenty yards the surface of the water is smooth, just a few long straight ripple-lines like silk pulled taut, before the slight breeze can catch at the water and fuzz it up like static. Further out, three small figures are paddleboarding their way towards Leasowe beach, as though giving us a line to follow.

Leasowe. It's the name Lowry uses in the beautiful passage in the first chapter of *Under the Volcano*, describing the setting for Jacques' and Geoffrey's first experience of both friendship and betrayal:

And that was how M. Laruelle came to Leasowe.

It was a kind of grown-up, civilized version of Courseulles on the English north-west coast. The Taskersons lived in a comfortable house whose back garden abutted on a beautiful, undulating golf course bounded on the far side by the sea. It looked like the sea; actually it was the estuary, seven miles wide, of a river: white horses westward marked where the real sea began. The Welsh mountains, gaunt and black and cloudy, with occasionally a snow peak to remind Geoff of India, lay across the river. During the week, when they were allowed to play, the course was deserted: yellow ragged sea poppies fluttered in the spiny sea grass. On the shore were the remains of an antediluvian forest with ugly black stumps showing, and farther up an old stubby deserted lighthouse. There was an island in the estuary, with a windmill on it like a curious black flower, which you could ride out to at low tide on a donkey. The smoke of freighters outward bound from Liverpool hung low on the horizon. There was a feeling of space and emptiness.

The passage goes on to mention the 'hydropathic hotels' and the marine lake. Lowry is, in fact, conflating various locations in this description. The hotels, the marine lake, the view across to Wales and to the island belong to West Kirby, a mile or so down the west coast of the Wirral. The remains of the submerged forest run along most of the northern Wirral coast, but are particularly concentrated around Meols. The golf course – though there is a links at Leasowe – is more closely based on the Royal Liverpool course at Hoylake, which forms a rough triangle in the corner of the peninsula and therefore looks both northwards, straight out to sea, and westerly across the Dee. Lowry creates a kind of composite image, a superimposition, for artistic purposes; and he chooses for it the name Leasowe.

As Bryan and I walk down onto Leasowe beach, I'm

wondering why I'd never really explored this place before this summer. I'd always taken the train to the end of one or other of the lines, rather than coming to this in-between place. I hadn't realised that it was a good place for walking, that you could follow the coast, along the strip of common or down on the sands, all the way to Red Rocks, about six miles, and then round the point and along to West Kirby. And I hadn't realised that there was a real beach here at Leasowe, almost a bay, held between two stone breakwaters, and even now in early November there are two people swimming, and a woman riding a horse slowly across the beach from east to west. The water is blue and flat calm, the sky blue but hazy, beginning to glow low down in the west behind the concrete embankment. The scene feels suspended: it's impossible to say what time of day or what month it is. It's not clear what time has passed since we were here in August or since I came here again in late September. Or we could be back further than that, back in the spring, when everything first changed and we wondered what it would mean.

Bryan and I sit on the rocks and I start taking off my boots. Are you kidding, he says. But I want at least to touch the water, to have some kind of encounter with it. The sand is cold but the water, when I reach it, is colder. The ache starts almost at once in the soft part of my feet, just below the arches, and spreads out as though following the paths of the bones, so that I keep picking my feet up out of the water as I walk, and I think of Bishop's description in 'At the Fishhouses', 'If you should dip your hand in, / your wrist would ache immediately, / your bones would begin to ache and your hand would burn / as if the water were a transmutation of fire'. Back on the rock, though, drying off my feet with the sleeve of my cardigan, it feels good to have done it, to have had the encounter, however brief.

As we walk up the shallow flights of steps set into the revetment, and round the point, the afternoon is definitely ending, the light beginning to fail, the sky ahead of us to the west now bands of pinkish-grey cloud, and the blue above darkening. Along at our left runs a fence, wire mesh strung between concrete posts, frayed and torn away in parts, suggesting some kind of military site now unimportant or forgotten. After a while it gives way to open land, and beyond that a straggling row of houses, pointing our way to the station and back to Liverpool.

Memorialising Rabindranath Tagore in Brighton

JOE WINTER

In 1878 a 17-year-old Bengali boy spent a short while at a school in Ship Street in Brighton. His father had sent him to England to study for the bar and he began his stay at an elder brother's home in Medina Villas (exact number not known). Very soon he went to London, where he spent a further year learning a great deal, but without surrendering to the rigours of a formal academic institution. The boy had walked out of his Kolkatan (then Calcuttan) school at the age of fourteen, and backed wholeheartedly by a rich and intellectually wide-ranging household full of wonderfully gifted elder brothers, had simply found his own way.

He became India's first winner of a Nobel Prize (in Literature in 1913), an internationally known writer in several genres, a composer of many hundreds of songs that have long been a mainstay of the Bengali world, an advocate for Indian Independence as famous as Gandhi up and down his land; and through his unending and passionate commitment to a forward-looking spirit of humanity across the continents, he became and still is a world-figure.

On 28 October 2021 a blue plaque recording his stay at the Brighton Proprietary School was unveiled at 7 Ship Street on the building that had housed the school. Some two hundred-odd people thronged the narrow road. India and Bangladesh, whose national anthems were played (both from songs composed by Tagore), were well represented; many were in national dress; there was a feeling, in the blowy air, with seagulls squawking and at times almost drowning out the various speeches being made, of something very Tagorean. As it happens the unveiling of the plaque coincided with the centenary of the birth of one of his deepest commitments.

Always engaged in social reforms for his land, in 1921 the poet set up a university in a village in Bengal and chose for its motto a Vedic text, 'Where the world makes its home in a single nest'. Said the founder, 'Visva-Bharati acknowledges India's obligations to offer the hospitality of her best culture and India's right to accept from others their best'. Visva-Bharati University still upholds the Tagorean ideal, as does the school Patha Bhavana he founded in the same village of Santiniketan twenty years before in 1901, where lessons are still held in the open (weather permitting), and where I am glad to have taught. In a present-day gathering intimately associated with the memory of the Indian polymath, as the plaque calls him, something intangible seemed to be re-captured for a moment. It cannot be named but it has to do with the acknowledgement of a free exchange of what matters most. For a moment the nest was in Britain in a small road.

How can one pin down the sense of freedom that can come to one from an idea of the works and days of Rabindranath Tagore? A visionary and a man of action, a maker of dreams and a taker of initiatives, he epitomises the creative current. It's good to think of the boy he was savouring the air and drifting along, in the early stages of becoming the independent individual he was to be, by the seagulls and the sea.

Letter from Wales

SAM ADAMS

M. Wynn Thomas, *Eutopia: studies in Cultural Euro-Welshness, 1850-1980*; and *The History of Wales in Twelve Poems* (both University of Wales Press, 2021), £24.99 and £8.99

Wynn Thomas has long since consolidated his position as the foremost interpreter of Welsh writing in English. He is principled, keenly perceptive and precise in judgement, and his writing is as elegant as it is clear, while pulling no punches. He is equally at home discussing the literature and history of Wales in the Welsh language, bringing to this field, too, the same rare qualities of wide knowledge, clarity and discrimination. These, his most recent books, are different in scope and intention from the twenty or so volumes that preceded them. They go far beyond 'lit. crit.' and confirm his standing among the foremost cultural historians of Wales.

Eutopia is a survey with parameters both chronological and geographical. It proposes that, compared to the reach and depth of the (lately American accented) anglophone penetration of much of the world by military and mercantile predation, Welsh connections with Europe, though they go back to the 'Age of the Saints', the *Mabinogion* and the poetry of Dafydd ap Gwilym, only multiply about the middle of the nineteenth century, and even since then 'cannot but seem piddling, provincial and hopelessly naive'. Thomas's assessment is, as ever, clear-sighted. Nevertheless, he insists, they have 'compelling power and continuing relevance', manifested not in politics, economics or mass movements (least of all tourist travel), but in the life experience of individuals, the intellectual elite who are the subject of his book. I can only be selective in giving a flavour of it.

During the latter part of the nineteenth century and deep into the twentieth, while the Welsh language was being undermined and eroded by denigration from without and doubt within, certain individuals were making their way through the English-language education system to positions that afforded them opportunities for European travel. With the odd exception, these bright emissaries were mostly from among the working class or at best the middling sort. O M Edwards (1859-1920) was among these pioneers. The son of a tenant farmer from Llanuwchlyn, near Bala, he overcame the setback of early schooling in a strange tongue to make his way, via Aberystwyth, Glasgow University and a prizewinning career at Balliol, to become a Fellow and tutor in history at Lincoln College, Oxford. Among his many publications were books about his travels in Europe designed for popular appeal – and written in Welsh. I have a particular regard for him as the first appointed chief inspector of schools in Wales in 1907, in which capacity he ensured all our schools taught Welsh. Similar histories, mostly of men, committed to exploring Europe from 'West to East' from 'Spain to Scandinavia', and bringing home the stimulating essence of their experience, reiterate the argument for cultural retention. Welsh is a European language, with standing among its fellows; to sink them all in Anglo-American is to abandon thousands of years of distinctive usefulness and beauty.

One outlier was a refugee from Germany shortly before the war. Kate Bosse-Griffiths (1910-98), born in Wittenberg of part-Jewish parents, had an exceptional academic career, was fluent in Italian and Russian, and (in Thomas's words) 'had mastered' Greek, Latin, Egyptian, Coptic, Classical Arabic and Hebrew. She met her husband, J Gwyn Griffiths (1911–2004), at Oxford, where he was studying Egyptology and she was a curator at the Ashmolean. She soon added Welsh to her array of languages and emerged as an accomplished writer of articles, short stories and novels that distinguish her as a proto-feminist, one of the first to bring the essential character of women's experience to Welsh language literature. Marriage took the couple to a house named 'Cadwgan' on the hillside above the mining village of Pentre in the Rhondda and, it seems to me, right to the heart of the book. There, still in the war years, Kate and her husband, by then a poet and distinguished scholar (later professor of Classics and Egyptology at Swansea) established, on European lines, a salon of young intellectuals, *Cylch Cadwgan,* the Cadwgan Circle. The membership included Rhydwen Williams (1916–97), a Baptist minister, who later twice won the Crown at the National Eisteddfod, wrote a trilogy of novels about the south Wales coalfield and became a notable figure in Welsh-language television; and Pennar Davies (1911–96), the gifted son of a Mountain Ash miner's family, who had an outstanding university career at Cardiff, Glasgow, Balliol and Yale, before returning to Oxford to study theology, preparatory to ordination as a Congregational minister. Astonishingly, Gareth Alban Davies (1926–2009), joined this group as a sixth former, spent three years in the mines as a Bevin Boy and, via Queen's, Oxford, became a lecturer and, in due course, professor of Spanish at Leeds University. A busy writer and translator, and an under-rated poet, he viewed the Spanish scene through Welsh eyes, and linked the threats to the Welsh language with those to Catalan. Discussion within the circle ranged widely over the history and culture of Europe and, notwithstanding the strong ministerial presence, was remarkably unfettered by prevailing polite convention. Some absorbing work arose from it, including Pennar Davies's novel of ideas, *Meibion Darogan* (1968), which Thomas identifies as 'the work of a European intellectual in search of an answering Welsh intelligentsia', and a group collection of poems, *Cerddi Cadwgan* (1953).

The Cadwgan group broke up when, at the end of the war, the Griffithses decamped to Bala. There they met Euros Bowen (1904–88), a native of Treorci, just a few miles up the Rhondda Fawr from Pentre. He was another who had trodden an unusual path through higher education, from Aberystwyth to Swansea and thence first to Mansfield and then St Catherine's, Oxford. He had also set out Nonconformist and ended Anglican. Rectory-bound in the ghastly winter of 1947, he began writing poems, quite extraordinary poems, owing a great deal more to the French symbolist poets than to the traditional forms and subject matter of Welsh poetry. He denied the link, referring to himself as a 'Christian Sacramentalist', although in 1980 he published *Beirdd Simbolaidd Ffrainc* (French Symbolist Poets), a collection of 'masterly translations' (Thomas's assessment) from Baudelaire, Malarmé, Rimbaud, Verlaine, Laforgue, Valéry and Claudel, which reveal his familiarity with the taint of Decadence. Reading *Poems* (1974), where the Welsh stands alongside his own English translations, we begin to grasp how, for him, 'the intermingling of the senses enables unique symbolic apprehension of the secret underlying unity of all creation':

Gwelais flodyn yr haul fy hun mewn gardd, a llygad
yn ei ben, yn gweld i'r byw:
Fel emosiwn melyn ar donnau glas y coed: fel
cragen yn gwrando am berlau llymeirch
    yn y mor ...
(I myself saw a sunflower in a garden, a bloom of
eyes penetrating the heart:
Like a yellow emotion on the blue waves of trees:
like a seashell intent on oystered

pearls ...)

If we follow Sir Thomas More, 'Eutopia' means 'good place'. Here it is a portmanteau into which are also packed the ideal civilized world of 'Utopia' and the abbreviation 'EU'. There are not many who would for a moment contemplate writing a compendious study of Welsh-European connections, fewer still capable of bringing it off. *Eutopia* might be considered a long lament for a lost cause; I prefer to think of it as a timely reminder of the heritage now slipping away from us, that just might galvanise efforts to hold on.

If the scope and thumping magnitude of *Eutopia* is the chief manifestation of this, *The History of Wales in Twelve Poems*, with illustrations by Ruth Jen Evans, is the nimble outrider, in essence, continuing the scholar's protest against the breaking of ancient ties, the closing of doors. The concept of the twelve-poem history could well have hatched from contemplation of Menna Elfyn's 'Siapiau o Gymru' (Shapes of Wales) – a mapped outline of the country that to a foreign student resembled 'a pig running away', but in the mind's eye of the poet is a boomerang, stubbornly returning again and again to her feet. The same helplessness lies at the heart T H Parry-Williams's 'Hon': 'mi glywaf grafangau Cymru'r dirdynnu fy mron;/Duw a'm gwaredo, ni allaf dianc rhag hon.' (I feel the claws of Wales rending my breast; God save me, I cannot escape from her.) But this is an increasingly uncommon response at the end of what Wynn Thomas characterises as 'long centuries of subordination, marginalisation and assimilation'.

Translating Dante

ALBERTO MANGUEL

Ned Denny, *B: After Dante* (Carcanet) £18.99

How much do poets know about their own creations? Other than post-partum rationalisations such as Poe's 'Philosophy of Composition' or Coleridge passing on the blame to the Person from Porlock, there are not many confessions of how the trick works, and even these are rarely convincing, maybe because deep down inside every bard is in fact a doubting, doubtful craftsperson with little or no idea of how this creation thing came about. Dante, however, was clearly aware of what he was accomplishing as he was working on his *Commedia*. Rarely was a poet so conscious of his craft, of how his thoughts were faithfully incarnated in his words, both as sense and as sound. I can't think of any other poet who with such hubris dares us, his readers, to follow him on the sea of invention and discovery that he is himself fording for the first time, while proudly telling us to 'wheel about' because our puny crafts (except for a few happy ones) cannot cross the ocean he is about to cross: 'Do not set out,' he warns us at the beginning of *Paradiso*, 'on depths where, losing me, you'll lose yourselves.' What poetic chutzpah, what absolute confidence in the poetic art, are necessary to tell us, as Dante does, that he's received among the inhabitants of the Noble Castle of the First Circle of Hell –Homer, Horace, Lucan, Ovid, Virgil himself—who anoint him 'sixth of their sage company'? And this only four cantos into the poem that with circular logic will prove the truth of this colossal assertion. That is not all. Dante tests the reader further, by swearing 'by the verses of his *Commedia*' that what

he will describe next (in Canto XVII of *Inferno*) –the appearance of monstrous allegory of fraud– is true. So we are left with this conundrum: either we believe in the truth of the preceding cantos, so convincing in their beauty and poetic honesty, and thereby accept the truth of fraud (material and imaginative fraud, i.e. counterfeiting and fiction) or we stop reading and close the book. '*Errori non falsi*' ('not untrue inventions') Dante calls them later on, in the sense that Cocteau defined himself as 'a lie that tells the truth.' In this complex maze of fictive story and deeply honest meaning that demands that we believe six impossible things before breakfast – what should the reader, even the best of readers, do?

Translators are (must be) among the best of readers. They cannot merely skim the surface of the text, or appropriate it as their personal looking-glass. They must pull the text apart, change the tone and connotation into whatever other language they are translating, and reassemble the whole lot as something that is and is not a faithful rendering of the original. Every text depends on the vocabulary, cultural landscape, musicality, grammar and syntax of the language in which it is composed, and is born from the ideas and images that this particular language allows. Translators, obedient to the etymology of their title, must carry the dismembered text from one linguistic continent to another, and hope that in the new soil it will grow new branches and new fruit. Translators must know their text literally inside out, with a much more questioning and demanding eye than the author's. And if this feat is almost impossible in the case of any simple text, how inconceivably greater the difficulty becomes in the case of a text such as the *Commedia,* rigorously constructed in a new tongue (Tuscan) and with a new rhyming scheme (*terza rima*), dependent of a numerological code as strict as any gematria, bound to a theological framework that must dialogue with the revealed wisdom of the Fathers of the Church, and subject to historical, mythological, astronomical, astrological, botanical, zoological, and literary givens written out in the obligatory library of a fourteenth-century European scholar. How to accomplish such a feat in a language such as English with different scansion, syllabic stress, religious dogma, historical references, music? A translator's ambition sometimes rivals that of a poet, and many have attempted the impossible. Since the first published translation in 1782 of *Inferno* in blank verse by Charles Rogers, and the first translation of the entire *Commedia* three years later by Henry Boyd, in rhymed 6-lined stanzas for the original rhymed tercets, to the latest ones many translators into the English language have dared to split the infinitive and to boldly go where many have gone before. Today, English can boast of more translations of the *Commedia* than any other language.

Like the perfect boiling of an egg for Cordon Bleu chefs, the translation of the first line of the *Commedia* is the determining test of a translator's ability. '*Nel mezzo del cammin di nostra vita*' is a perfect summation of the poem, with echoes of the incipit of Psalm 113, '*In exitu Israel de Egipto*' in reference the 'three-score years and ten' allotted to us in Psalm 90. It conjures up the ancient image of the road of life, and introduces the first-person singular narrator (the Pilgrim) included in the plural '*nostra*'. There is plenty more to discover in those first seven words, but these echoes will suffice for a comparison.

The first two English translators were variously conscious of these connotations. Charles Rogers wrote:

When in my middle Stage of Life, I found
Myself entangl'd in a wood obscure...

Henry Boyd:

When life had labour'd up her midmost stage,
And, weary with her mortal pilgrimage...

The chasm between Rogers' interpretation and Boyd's is unbreachable. These first two intrepid explorers of Dante's road of life see it, the first, as a piecemeal gradient, the second as the protagonist of the pilgrimage. Dante, of course, stated it as a simple, commonplace image that, in the allegorical reading, becomes Life itself (as the road travelled, not the traveller) and in the literal reading, the commencement of the journey.

A little over a century later, in 1908, H. F. Cary, translating against Boyd, wrote in plain English:

In the midway of this our mortal life,

I found me in a gloomy wood, astray.

The twenty-first century, perhaps with an eye on the seventh centennial of Dante's death celebrated this year, saw a deluge of Dante translations concocted by poets, scholars, academics and mere *apassionati* that attempted to find in post-Reformation English a tongue that would adequately echo Dante's endemic Florentine. A few of the productions were honourable and pleasing, many were not and resembled in their inadequacy those curious versions of European films 'translated' by Hollywood for American audiences.

One of latest versions of the *Commedia* to land on my desk was the oddly titled *B* by Ned Denny, subtitled *after Dante* to help unimaginative readers such as myself understand what they are about to read. The 'B' as the reader discovers is justified by the nomenclature chosen by Denny for the three parts of the poem: 'Blaze' for *Inferno*, 'Bathe' for *Purgatorio*, and 'Bliss' for *Paradiso*. Puzzling choice, but modestly justified since the familiarity of twenty-first century English-language audience, by and large, is limited to horror films and video games for the first part, practically nothing for the second, and to chains of sex shops for the third.

Denny is a poet deeply conscious of the limitations and riches of the English language, and its differences with Italian. While Italian verse is accentual and syllabic, mostly choosing feminine rhymes over masculine ones, and prefers the hendecasyllable for its verse (as in the *Commedia*), English verse prefers the iambic pentameter, where the pattern of stressed and unstressed syllables creates the metre, slightly varying certain parts of the line of verse. In most Latin languages, the stress sequence is quite regular, with the stress commonly falling on the tenth syllable. In Italian, for instance, metre is formed by a pattern of long and short vowels, and is determined merely by the position of the last accent in a line of verse; when a word ends with a vowel and the next one starts with a vowel, both are considered part of the same syllable (for example, '*Gli anni e i giorni*' consists of four syllables: '*Gli an-*' '*-ni e i' gior-*' and '*-ni'.*) Taking all this into consideration, Denny explains his method: 'Rather than ape the *Commedia*'s outward form, I have aimed to create a living equivalent different from but parallel to the highly structured and numerologically-minded original. Each of B's nine hundred stanzas is a roughly 12 by 12 block, the ground plan of the Book of Revelation's radiant 'foursquare' city' line-lengths vary but no stanza falls short of or exceeds 144 syllables, this number evoking both the 144,000 who 'sung as it were a new song' and the hours in the six days of Creation (and thus the end and the beginning of sacred time). With the addition of the single hanging line with which each canto opens and closes, this gives a total of 11,000 lines for the whole poem – transposing, in a sense, Dante's hendecasyllable onto the vertical plane.'

The result is a perfect blend of poetic inspiration, structural discipline and common sense. Of course, Denny's translation, with all the good will in the world, cannot be called literal. It is however, I believe, faithful to Dante. These are the first two lines:

In the midst of the stroll of this life that some call
  good
I came to my senses in a corpse-hued wood,

'Stroll' is a strange choice for Dante's '*cammin*' changing the passive 'road' or 'path' for the active 'stroll' that demands someone to undertake the action. 'Some call good' is not in Dante. And yet, it might be assumed that the Epicurean notion of a materially-enjoyable life (that Dante will see condemned in the circle of the heretics, those '*che l'anima col corpo morta fanno*' which Denny reads as those 'whose spiel was a myopic creed of the mortal soul') is present in Dante's vision of our error-laden earthly path of life; if so, it is deeply buried in the adjectiveless 'nostra vita' and Denny has boldly mined it. '*Mi retrovai*' translated into 'I came to my senses' is exactly right. The verb '*retrovarsi*' means 'to find oneself in a certain place': surely the physical idea of location can be extended, profitably, to the notion of the sudden illumination necessary to initiate the forthcoming pilgrimage. And 'corpse-hued' for '*oscura*' is most probably what Dante had in mind: the dark night of the soul lost in the dark wood of sin whose wages are death. One could go on.

In a 1932 essay on the translations of Homer, Borges suggested that a translation is merely another draft of the original: he added that the various drafts of a text can be regarded as 'translations into the same language'. The biography of a text can therefore be seen as the succession of drafts, translations included, which add to or subtract something from the supposed original. (Borges also said that the notion of a definitive text can belong only to religion or fatigue.) If this is so, then translators have the choice of several strategies. They can attempt to be faithful to the text both in sense and sound, but in doing so risk betraying the text through that very faithfulness by introducing novelties and artifice that may be absent in the original language, because what is natural in one tongue might be startling or unconvincingly odd in another.

I believe that a translation must, like Borges' draft, stand on its own and require the comparison with the distant original. Every reading is an interpretation, every interpretation effects a change that requires a new reading and allows for a new interpretation. A translation is not a many-layered Troy that Schliemann discovered and that successive archaeologists have dug out in search of the authentic Ilion known to Helen. Somewhere in the distance, between the lines of Denny's *B: After Dante*, lies Dante's *Commedia*: unscathed, immaculate, perfect as perhaps no other work of literature. To look for archaeological precision, to demand from the translation the exactitude required in a document as proof of identity, is to mistake the role of the reader for that of the philological censor. Denny is certainly not Dante, *B* is certainly not the *Commedia*, but (in the eyes of this reader at least) *B* is one of the best versions of the great poem I have read, and Denny has written a great English-language poem in its own right.

'On Finding a Horseshoe' *often translated as* 'The Horseshoe Finder'

(Pindaric Fragment)

OSIP MANDELSTAM

translated from the Russian by Sasha Dugdale

We look at the wood and we say:
  – There's a shipwright's forest, a forest of masts,
Pink pines,
Free from the mass of fronds to their very tips
They ought to be creaking in gales
Singly, stone pines,
In the fury of a treeless sky,
Resisting the salt heel of the wind,
a plumb line driven into the dancing deck,
And the seafarer
In his unquenchable thirst for the expanse
Hauls the geometer's delicate instruments
                          through watery valleys,
Measuring, against the drag of the earth's hold,
The shivering surface of the seas.
And breathing in the smell

Of resinous tears, seeping through the
                          ship's planking,
Admiring the boards
Clinched down, laid into bulwarks
Not by the gentle Bethlehem carpenter, but another
The father of travel, a friend to the seafarer –
We say:
They too once stood on the earth
The awkward earth, like the spine of a mule
And their tips have forgotten their roots
On that famed mountain ridge
Where they whisper under freshwater downpours
Asking the unheeding sky to exchange their noble
                          freight
For a thimble of salt.

Where to start?
Everything shudders and sways
The air trembles with comparisons.
No single word is better than another,
The earth hums with metaphor
And light chariots
In the flashing harness of throngs of birds, taut with
   the strain,
Break apart
Competing with the snorting favourites of the
   tiltyards.

Thrice blessed he who introduces name into his
   song
For the song beautified by name
Will live longer among the others –

She, alone of her friends, wears a bandage on her
   brow
To cure her of forgetting, that overly strong
                              intoxicating scent
Like the proximity of a man
Or the coat of a powerful beast
Or the perfume of savoury, rubbed between the
   palms.

The air is sometimes dark, like water, and all the
living
                              swim in it, like fish
Fins forcing forward, shoving
The taut-skinned, solid, slightly warm sphere,
A crystal, in which wheels turn and horses shy
Neaera's moist black soil, nightly
                              tilled anew
With forks, tridents, hoes and ploughshares.
The air as densely-fleshed as the earth:
You can't leave, you can barely enter.
A shiver moves through the trees like a green oar
Children play at knucklebones with the vertebrae
                              of dead animals.
The fragile calendar of our era draws
                              to its close.
Thank you for what has passed:
I was mistaken, I strayed, I lost count.
The era clinked like a golden ball,
Cast in a round, supported by no hand,
Answering every touch with *yes* and *no*.
Like a child might say:
I'll give you an apple, or *I won't give it you*

And the child's face like a cast made from the voice
                              uttering these words.
The sound rings on, but the source of the sound is
   gone.
The horse lies in the dust, and snorts and foams
But the sharp twist of his neck
Still carries the memory of the race
                              legs flung wide –
Not just four of them,
But as many as stones on the road,
Starting afresh every four beats
The number of strikes made on the earth
                              by the steaming horse.
So, when he finds the horseshoe
Blows the dust from it
Wipes it with wool, till it shines
Then
Hangs it over the threshold,
So it can breathe deep
Never again will it be made to shear sparks
                              from the flint.
Human lips with nothing more to say
Hold the shape of the last word,
And the hand still knows the sensation of weight
Although the jug has spilled half its load
                              on the way home.

That which I say now, is not spoken by me –
It is scraped from the ground like fossilised grains
                              of wheat.
Some
      inscribe lions on their coins,
Others
      a head.
All the various rounds of copper, gold
                              bronze
Lie with equal honour in the ground,
The age bites down on them, leaving the marks
                              of its teeth.
Time clips me, like a coin.
And I have already felt the loss of myself.   1923

This translation will appear in The Art of the Russian
Poem, 1918–2018 *published by Princeton University Press
in 2022.*

A Note on Mandelstam's 'The Horseshoe Finder'

ANDREW KAHN

The poetry of *Stone* (1910), Osip Mandelstam's first collection, was about poetic craft and self-discovery. In *Tristia* (1923), his second collection, Mandelstam became a full-fledged Modernist. Like Eliot, he was a poet of retrieved culture, allusive and layered, and like Yeats he was under the spell of the Golden Bough. The tumult of history does not register in these books. Yet Mandelstam and History had one another in view. He faced the new reality of the Russian Revolution head on in the great historical poems he published separately in the early Soviet press. Inspired by a fin-de-siècle and Nietzschean vision of destruction and renewal, he made his poetry new by writing on a larger scale about the perishability and survival of culture and the dawning of new poetic consciousness. 'The Age' (1918) confronts the violence needed to kill off the old. The 'Slate Ode' (1922) takes civilization back to a primitive state to refashion the consciousness of a nation. 'Paris' (1923) interrogates the laws of history to see whether the French Revolution had already scripted Russia's destiny. Who could see far enough into the future or into the past to predict the outcome? The vatic speaker has a new song to sing. The reader experiences Orphic-sounding mystery, hidden and found objects, talismanic words, incantatory song

Mandelstam is by and large a stanzaic poet. 'The Horseshoe Finder' consists of unrhymed blank verse, and its blocks of lines are demarcated by rhetorical questions, exclamations, and repetition. Its sudden shifts, collapse of horizontal and vertical planes and prominent first-person give it a Futurist dynamism worthy of Mayakovsky. It has an imagistic and metaphorical extravagance fully justifying the allusion to Pindar in the sub-title, combining the seafaring of the Argonauts and the Olympic horse-race. Here a tree has already been built proleptically from the forest, a plumbline fixes its compass for the navigator or geometer, who navigates a sea whose roughness has the texture of the forest. It is no wonder that well after the poem has sketched the shipbuilding plan the speaker notes that the 'air vibrates from comparisons' (l.31). And in the manner of the Pindaric ode, the circumstances of the poem's production animate the poet: the poet must build his own craft in order to navigate the torrent of the age. Like the Olympic athlete of the Pindaric ode, the contestant seeks a prize. 'Thrice-blessed is he who leads a name into the song' is that goal. 'How the ship was built, of what materials, how it was launched, and how the poem as a song was sung become completely intertwined. Matching music and vision, the poem finds a propulsive rhythm on which to launches the ship's journey. Sasha Dugdale's translation conveys both the massiveness and vision and velocity of thought, her version of nearly every phrase

also syntactically and sonically close to the original. To take one example: 'the salt heel of the wind' (l. 8) transfers not only the exact words but also the sound of the words. Sometimes called a philological poet, Mandelstam held that the shape of the word, its aural envelope or the 'cast made from the voice uttering these words', was part of its meaning. That the 'sound rings on' in English is a mark of the quality of this version.

'The Horseshoe Finder' is Mandelstamian version of Rimbaud's ('Le Bateau ivre'). Both inspired poet-sailors abandon their ships: Rimbaud's to interrogate the skies for their future vital energy ('ô future Vigueur'), Mandelstam to excavate the earth and ponder the found object buried in the earth and layers of time. The poet starts as an Argonaut, then moves forward on a ship pulled by sparrows, a passenger of Aphrodite or Apollo, and then finally seems to move through the air and the sea as an Olympian contestant on some marvellous amphibious craft, ploughing both realms simultaneously.

The poet-seafarer launched into the unknown. Once the ship itself has come into existence the speaker stands back to admire a vessel that has not been built by a 'peaceful carpenter of Bethlehem', suggesting that History has turned away from a Judaeo-Christian future. The historically distanced poet distils experience of the journey and confusion into aphorism: 'No single word is better than another' (l.34), 'The fragile calendar of our era draws to a close' (l.62), 'The sound rings on, but the source of the sound is gone' (l.73). Self-awareness coincides with the acknowledgement of a shift from mythic time to historical time. If the world was golden, turning at that point in a historical cycle, that might mean it was golden by privilege of being first in a sequence that inevitably brought decline. But even a golden age, now seen retrospectively, seems to have involved guilt. The speaker's attitude is marked by reckoning (l. 58), by confession of right and wrong, and by childlike snippets of speech that record acts of gift-giving that belong to the child or humanity in its infant state. Was it wrong to launch forth? 'For everything that has been/thank you' gives the answer. It may also convey elegiacally a farewell to an earlier time, and an earlier self, whose echoes reverberate. Has the ship headed in the wrong direction? If the speaker loses the assurance of the geometer, his visionary elan still gives confidence: 'Thrice blessed he who introduces name into his song/ For the song beautified by name/Will live longer among the other' (l.40). Survival of the name all depends on the reader aka horseshoe finder able to decipher the marks left in the historical and geological record—but, above all, to read the marks left on the language by the poet.

Of the Hermit Crab and other poems

ROMULO BUSTOS AGUIRRE

Translated from the Colombian Spanish by Richard Gwyn

Ballad of the House

You will find a house with a strange name
    that you will attempt in vain to decipher
And walls the colour of good dreams
But you will not see that colour
Nor will you drink the red plum wine
    that stretches memories

On the gate
sits a child with a half-open book
Ask him the way to the big trees
whose fruits are guarded by an animal
that sends passers-by to sleep just by looking at them
And he will answer while conversing
    with a green-winged angel
(as if it were another child playing at being an angel
with wide banana leaves stuck to his back)

barely moving his lips in a gentle spell
    'the cockerel's song isn't blue but a sleepy pink
    like the first light of day'

And you will not understand. Nevertheless
you will find an immense hallway
where hangs the portrait of a lord,
    shimmering slightly, his heart in his hand
and at the back, right at the back
the soul of the house seated in a rocking chair, singing
but you will not heed her

because in that instant
a distant sound shall crease the horizon
and the child will have finished the last page

Of the Hermit Crab

Strange, the ways of the hermit crab

He gets by in life looking for the shells of other
molluscs, tins, empty receptacles,
every kind of concave object abandoned
by their previous guests, and installs himself in them

It's possible that this is due to a touristic compulsion for
    novelty
Or to an almost metaphysical insecurity syndrome

Or a simple peripatetic exercise
for one who has too many legs to exercise

Or might there be something more at the bottom of all
    this?

Perhaps it would be worth asking
the secret hermit crab that inhabits
each one of us

The one who, no doubt, has just written this poem

Marbella Scene

To Juan Marchena, Cartagenina
from the other side of the sea

Near the rocks, belly up, is God
The fishermen in a line heave at the net
And now he lies there, white eyes staring at the sky
He looks like a terminally distracted swimmer
He looks like a big fat fish with a very big tail
But it's only God
swollen up and with spoiled scales
How much time has he pitched across the waters?
The curious observe the monstrous catch
Some of them cut off a slab and carry it back
    to their houses
    Others wonder if it would be advisable
to eat something that has spent so much time
    exposed to the elements.

Story

I ask myself: why do I write poetry?
And from some place in the mysterious forest
(in that other story that I am trying in vain
    to write with this poem)
the wolf replies
with a Socratic movement of his bushy tail:

– The better to know you.

Seeing through the Words

JENNY LEWIS

The Imagist poet H.D. said, of her translations of Euripides, 'I know that we need scholars to decipher the Greek but that we also need poets and mystics... to see through the words.'[1] George Steiner agrees, arguing in the introduction to his book *After Babel* (1998) that it is 'creative' translations, by translators who do not necessarily speak the source language but are poets, novelists or dramatists in their own right, that can best preserve for posterity the 'possible worlds and geographies' that each language construes. Dryden defines this as 'paraphrase' but it is now generally described as 'creative' as opposed to 'literal' or 'word-for-word' translation. 'Creative' translation is increasingly encouraged, for example by the Stephen Spender Trust who offer 'Creative Translation in the Classroom' education programmes. It has also been validated for decades by translation theorists such as Lawrence Venuti who asserts that the source language poem is open to becoming just one of multiple equally acceptable variations. Yet 'creative' translation still has a substantial body of detractors. So why do so many poets risk opprobrium and strike out on their own to translate canonical texts without even the map and compass of knowing the language it is written in?

For Simon Armitage, the 'preposterous' conviction that he was put on earth to translate Gawain was prompted by co-incidence. In an article in the Guardian (16 December 2006) he explains how his wife's dog-eared copy of the Tolkien and Gordon edition of the Green Knight fell open at a particular page and his eye was attracted to the word 'wodwo'. Being a Hughes fan, he took this as a sign. He was then beset by doubts – wondering if he had the stamina, aptitude 'or even the right' to be 'fiddling around with this ancient text.' Among many reasons, including the fact that he himself is a Northerner, or North Midlander, as the original poet is thought to have been, he says the anonymity of the author seemed to 'serve as an invitation, opening up a space within the poem for a new writer to occupy'. Using Marie Borroff's translation alongside Tolkien's, he decided to imitate the highly alliterative form because he felt that the sense of the poem is located in the 'percussive patterning' of its sound. Ezra Pound's translations from Chinese, published in *Cathay* (1915) also came about by chance, in this case through meeting Ernest Fenollosa's widow at a London literary salon in 1913 who persuaded him to edit her husband's essay and notes 'The Chinese Written Character as a Medium for Poetry'. Even though he couldn't read or speak Chinese, the ideogrammatic nature of Chinese script chimed with his imagistic approach, inspiring a prolonged engagement with Chinese literature and leading T.S. Eliot to remark, in his introduction to Pound's *Selected Poems* (1948), that Pound was 'the inventor of Chinese poetry for our time'. When Seamus Heaney was commissioned to translate Beowulf for the *Norton Anthology of English Literature* he was tempted because, while he admitted to having 'no great expertise' in Old English, he wanted to get back to the 'first stratum' of language and 'assay the hoard'. After a false start when the slow, labour-intensive work started to defeat him, the project was shelved, to be taken up again and completed later because, he says, he was 'reluctant to abandon his own linguistic and literary origins.'[2]

In my own case, my longing to translate the world's oldest known piece of written literature, the *Epic of Gilgamesh,* began when I stumbled across it while researching my father's active service in the First World War Mesopotamian Campaign for my book, *Taking Mesopotamia* (2014). Collated from cycles of stories dating back to 2,500 BC, Gilgamesh was supposedly first written down in the form we know it by the priest/ scribe/ exorcist Sin-leque-uninni in around 1200 BC. The ancient culture it derived from is still so relevant to 21st century concerns that Gilgamesh, with his friends and enemies, gods and goddesses, strode into my mind with the colossal power of Wordsworth's mountain pursuing him across the moonlit lake. The tale of Gilgamesh, King of Uruk, himself so superbly alive, so catastrophically flawed, and of Enkidu the wild man, 'born from silence', the 'id' to Gilgamesh's 'ego', or a blank screen for the reader to project his or her own consciousness onto, became the bedrock for future epics (think Gilgamesh + Enkidu /Achilles + Patroclus, hero quests, interfering deities, journeys to the underworld) and had the same mesmerising effect on me as it had had on Rilke who, in a letter to Katherina Kippenberg, dated 11 December, 1916 said 'Gilgamesh is tremendous!' and that he counted it among the greatest texts that could be experienced. Gilgamesh, I found, flowed into me, filled me up and started leaking out everywhere. I wrote a play, *After Gilgamesh*, for Pegasus Theatre, Oxford (2012), a sequence of poems for *Taking Mesopotamia* and a festival theatre piece, *Gilgamesh Rising*; yet I still hadn't got Gilgamesh out of my system. So in 2013, encouraged by my editor at Oxford Poets/ Carcanet, Robyn Marsack, and despite the fact that I could neither read Babylonian nor decipher cuneiform, I set out to write a new 'creative' translation of Gilgamesh, *Gilgamesh Retold*, working mainly from Andrew George's 2003 Penguin version with recourse to several other versions and related literature.

At the same time I was working with the exiled Iraqi poet Adnan Al-Sayegh on translating extracts from his epic anti-war poem, *Uruk's Anthem*. With Adnan, whose English is limited (although better than my almost

---

1 Quoted in Josephine Balmer, *Piecing Together the Fragments: Translating Classical Verse, Creating Contemporary Poetry* (OUP, 2013).

2 Seamus Heaney, *Beowulf, a New Translation* (Faber, 1999).

non-existent Arabic), my methodology was different. We relied on bridge translations by nine different translators, one a gifted Palestinian-Lebanese student of mine, Ruba Abughaida, who worked on around one quarter of the text with us and was the only person we had a face-to-face session with. The others were mainly friends of Adnan who had helped in any way they could over the years. With these texts of markedly varying quality before us, we painstakingly worked our way through around 5,000 lines, 'poeticising' each word, image, colloquialism, surrealism, rhetorical figure and endnote. As the (seven) years went by I learned more about Arabic poetry and culture; and the more extracts we translated the better I began to understand the overarching patterns and symphonic qualities of the full text. Influenced by Adnan's own musical reading style, I shaped my translation in response, using my intuition as a poet and songwriter to find cadences that gave the words (now my words) their own, different drive, humour or pathos, evaluating success by the reaction and feedback from audiences. 'Now my words', I say, and I am reminded of William Moran's introduction to David Ferry's version of Gilgamesh, *Gilgamesh: A New Rendering in English* (1993), where he says 'Let it be stated at once: it is David Ferry's poem. It is not Sin-leqe-uninni's.' Like climbing mountains, it seems, poets are drawn to 'creative' translation of epic texts 'because they are there' and they want to bring to them their own unique gifts and skills as poets and stamp them as their own.

For all his admiration of Pound's Chinese translations, Eliot questioned the validity of foreign translations generally. While the Elizabethans 'must have thought they *got* Homer through Chapman...' he goes on to say in the same introduction, 'we have not that illusion; we see that Chapman is more Chapman than Homer.' He could have added that Pope is more Pope and Logue more Logue than Homer. All three of these celebrated translations were 'creative'. When Chapman started on the *Iliad* he knew only a little Greek. Twelve years later he had acquired, through Latin-Greek lexicons and other cribs, a much deeper knowledge of the language. So much so that he claimed to have been visited by Homer's ghost (on a hillside in Hitchin) who explained how he had 'invisibly' prompted Chapman 'To those fair Greens, where thou dids't English me'.[3] The great strength Chapman brought to his *Iliad* was his skill as a dramatist. His knowledge of theatre and ear for the spoken word gave him the authority and freedom to create a swashbuckling playwright's version, full of neologisms and tumbling enjambment where narrated speech was often transposed into fast-moving direct discourse. Pope's reasons for translating the *Iliad* were at least to some extent commercial. His publication of the work between 1715 and 1720 in six volumes by subscription, initially to an aristocratic readership, secured an income for him which allowed him to live on his own means as a professional author. He worked from bilingual editions, a 1699 French prose version by Madame Dacier and literal

translations provided by Oxford classicists Elijah Fenton and William Broome. Pope's distanced and painterly *Iliad* reflects his interest in classical architecture and the art of the landscape garden. He also brought to it a sense of decorum, funnelling its energies into heroic couplets and aestheticizing some of Homer's cruder passages. Aestheticizing is a strategy I also used to describe the week long sex marathon between Shamhat the temple prostitute (or *hierodule*) and Enkidu in *Gilgamesh Retold*, finding it hard to imagine a scenario where a woman would willingly trek three days into the wilderness and lie naked by a waterhole as bait for a huge wild man (wodwo?) covered in a pelt of black hair – unless forced. My solution was to make the episode into a cultic rite or 'offering' in honour of the sex goddess, Inanna.

Christopher Logue was first cajoled into translating an extract from the *Iliad* by Donald Carne-Ross for a BBC programme in 1959. He had no knowledge of Greek and was openly hostile to scholar-translators who did. Key to his version were his experience as a political activist and ex-soldier and his career as a scriptwriter for theatre and film. 'Picture the east Aegean sea by night' his poem starts. The next stanza continues with an imperative, followed by a stream of active verbs 'Now look...see/.../Run .../Then kneel ... burst into tears, and say "Mother, ..."'. The film directions continue throughout the poem. The relaxation of censorship in the 1960s and 70s, which led to Edward Bond's *Saved* at the National in 1965, where a baby is stoned on stage, and the popularity of 1970's films like Peckinpah's misogynistic *Straw Dogs* and Burgess/Kubrick's *A Clockwork Orange,* provided a comfortable climate for the relentless violence of Logue's *Iliad*.

Despite historic legitimacy and Lawrence Venuti, there is still a body of feeling that only linguists who can speak the foreign language are entitled to translate it. Eric Griffiths in his review of Sean O'Brien's *Dante's Inferno: A Verse Translation*, ('Down with the Damned', the *Guardian,* Saturday 9 December, 2006) says that there is nothing worse than 'remembering the felicity of Dante's lines while toiling through O'Brien's wretched stuff'. Yet some of the most lauded translations of the 21st century have been 'creative', with varying degrees of acknowledgement to the original author/s. For example, Don Paterson's *Orpheus*, translations of Rilke's 55 sonnets, is without attribution to Rilke on the front cover. The rest of us mostly legitimise our 'wretched stuff' by how we describe it. Of the *Iliad* we have 'accounts' (Logue), 'excavations' (Alice Oswald) and 'hauntings' (Michael Longley). Ferry calls his Gilgamesh a 'rendering'. I describe my Gilgamesh as a 'response' to the original epic, and a 'retelling'. Ted Hughes's 'retellings', which form a crucial part of his oeuvre, relied on bridge translations which he preferred to be as literal and unpolished as possible. A monolinguist, he used them to activate his own poetic imagination, flagging up the issue of how the practice of 'creative' translation is increasingly becoming a way for poets to energise their own practice and experiment with adopting new voices.

A few writers prefer to invent, rather than adopt, a voice and challenge themselves to fit an existing text onto an *avant garde* template. Louis Zukofsky's experiments with phonemic or homophonic poetry, for exam-

---

3 Quoted in Colin Burrow, 'Chapmaniac', 'Review of *Chapman's Homer: The Iliad*', *London Review of Books*, 27 June 2002.

ple, which extended to his translations of Catullus, and Philip Terry's version of Gilgamesh, *Dictator* (2018) which is written using the constraints of Globish, a vocabulary of business language assembled by the poet Jean-Paul Nerrière. My own version of Gilgamesh has been called feminist and disruptive of male narratives by reviews in the *New Yorker*, the *TLS* and elsewhere. Indeed, had it *not* been I suggest it would have been a dereliction of purpose. To not have focused on rehabilitating the archetypes of the goddess, the prostitute and the hero; to not have provided a more woman-friendly interpre-

tation of the predominantly macho Sin-leque-uninni text when I was writing from a literary aesthetic shaped by Virginia Woolf, Angela Carter, Adrienne Rich, *l'écriture féminine* and the #MeToo movement would have been a pointless exercise. As to my right to subject an iconic text to such individualistic treatment, I echo the 'partly naïve but helpful' statement that Armitage kept telling himself to help him quell his doubts while translating Gawain: 'this is a poem, and I am a poet. What other permission is needed?'

Thirteen Poems

ARMANDO URIBE

Translated from the Chilean Spanish by Neil Davidson

From *Los obstáculos* (1961)

Ruffled nightingale, rising
from earth to sing in the tree
and use it as your lyre, I dare you
to sing upon a stone, like me.

***

I have no background in farming
or garlands of daisies.
I was born on a white sheet
and weaned in a darkened room.

***

What is others' becomes ours
like well-worn shoes. Loneliness
buffs them to mauve, to lilac. Bare
soles of the feet, the walker's
bare thighs, fingers, nails, polished
teeth, damp lustrous hair!...
Yet – fatty food, rank
locks; the vinegary dressing's
burnt oil, the salt that freezes...

Shoes again, soles and tongues.

From *No hay lugar* (1971)

I would die if I could as I am now,
groomed and combed, in a suit
and waistcoat; but I shall die
naked, dishevelled; among others, one more.

From *Los ataúdes* (1999)

I sang, when I was young, of carrion.
Spoke of it, that is. As to what it was,
I had no notion. How time passes! And now
it is what I am beneath my mourning clothes.
(As though having once said: anacoluthon
I had become that. A 'poet's'
pernickety ways. It scares me.
Where my tomb was once, chicory, planted, grows).

From *Las críticas de Chile* (1999)

(From the section 'Criticisms of political life')

This is us now, in the mousetrap
of a country turned mangy cat
that lies in wait for us
to go up to the cheese and gnaw the rind
so it can fell us with one swipe to the neck

and eat us up, then off to the ossuary.

***

The dictatorship
was no mistake, it comes with surnames,
like rats' or lizards' tails,

and its roll of honour for murderers
rejoices them still and goes
on and on; no mix-up, then,
but just a willingness to grind
children down like iron.

***

The fools say in their hearts
'there is no God', and this discovery
in itself does secretly rejoice
their hearts. The fools think
– if they do think – that there is no God
and rub their hands in glee.

(From the section 'Criticisms of social life')

And what became
of that Chilean, a countryman,
cultured, virile, vernacular,
lord of a few acres,
acquainted with the laws,
unhurried? He is done with and shall be buried:

From *A peor vida*, 2000

Those who went with him
into the tunnel of the grave, where are they now? Kingly,
he had his pyre of grim young bodies. And that
was and is as it should be. Cram them in
says the nameless hole. They bathed
in bloods and their name was one that is nameless.

no trains run now,
the iron shutters are coming down,
town and country are like a graveyard.

(From the section 'Criticisms of sexual life')

Cities intricate and secret,
and half-light in the upper storeys!
Books of Japanese prints,
Etchings on walls, and fans,
Velvet tassels and silken straps,
The great sloping mirror.
Bound at the wrists, bound by the feet.
A smile painful and violet with rouge.
And her crupper is a crowd of loves frisking
with sleek equine motions, a mane floating on breath.
Crime of virtue and delight of vice,
Broad violet blotches, bruises
most sweet, saliva like the juice
of seawater, jewels in silvered
rings, emphatic instruments
of torture, the sun will make us blind
with its lightning playing and its shattering flash.

From *De verso bruto*, 2002

(cf. Pascal, *Pensées*, 397 ff.
Port-Royal edition, III.
Man's shortcomings prove there must be a
    God – He has to exist.)

Look no further to prove
we are a fallen species
than the ignominy of the voided bowel.
Squatting, wiping, smells most foul!
The contemplation of faeces.
They are a proof of God greater than love.

***

For love of one who was divine
and yet by me made human rots
in a human grave I now repine.
She loves me loves me not not.
I love her though just rotting meat
wherein the bones are loosely bound.
I'll be a rodent in the ground,
be ashes, foetus, at her feet.

Often spoken of in Chile as the country's foremost living poet before his death in 2020 at eighty-six, Armando Uribe was also a lawyer and diplomat who helped draft the Treaty of Tlatelolco banning nuclear weapons in Latin America and rose to be director general of the diplomatic service. A supporter of the Allende government, he was ambassador in China at the time of Pinochet's coup and went into exile in France, where he taught political sciences at the Sorbonne and wrote the much-translated

Black Book of American Intervention in Chile, a study informed by an earlier spell in Washington. Back in Chile, he concluded that the country's new democracy was an 'infamous and fraudulent sell-out' that perpetuated the dictatorship and neoliberalism, and denounced all those complicit in it. They included everyone who might have given him a job, and he never held paid employment again. In 1998, after a son's death, he 'cloistered' himself in his flat to review his life and await his own end, while publishing profusely. His mixture of vitriol and Catholic orthodoxy, self-mockery and lawyerly pedantry, made him a favourite of interviewers, and he ended his life a household name.

If political polemic overshadowed Uribe's verse, he had no objection: 'In a country like this,' he commented late in life, 'to busy oneself putting words together in a way that might create some literary spark is a frivolous, shallow occupation for a grown man.' Yet he always wrote – quickly and impatiently, discarding whatever didn't work at the first attempt – and produced book after book of short lyrics, as well as political and autobiographical works, tracts on criminal and mining law and a novel. Often named as a member of Chile's 'generación literaria del 1950', he himself looked more to poets such as Montale, Ungaretti, Quasimodo, Pound (all of whom he translated) and Browning than to his own contemporaries. His subject-matter over more than half a century was consistent: death, despair, injustice, his own futility and folly, the difficulty and inevitability of belief in God, and his beloved wife Cecilia, the 'she' of the last of the poems translated here.

Of Making Books

ALASTAIR JOHNSTON

A Poetics of the Press: Interviews with Poets, Printers & Publishers, edited by Kyle Schlesinger (Cuneiform Press & Ugly Duckling Presse, 2021) $30

Kyle Schlesinger's book *A Poetics of the Press* contains sixteen interviews with small press publishers, mostly American, mostly letterpress printers, with one Briton (the late Tom Raworth) and one Kiwi, Alan Loney. It gives oral histories of American maverick small presses from Burning Deck to Effing Press. I am one of the interviewees, which perhaps should disqualify me from reviewing it, but I am consequently knowledgeable on the topic. There are threads that run through the book, from poets admired by all and published by some, to cultural figures (Charles Olson, Oprah!) and movements (Fluxus) that loom over many stories. Schlesinger doesn't miss opportunities and managed to get the recalcitrant Raworth to open up a bit about Barry Hall, with whom he co-published the American poets of the mid-century at Goliard Press in London in the '60s, and Asa Benveniste, expatriate American who was art director of Studio Vista and publisher of the superlative Trigram Press in London at the same time. But Raworth speaks elliptically so it helps to know his biography. A typical Raworth response is this exchange:

Michael Cross: Are you working on anything now?
TR: In the sense that I'm always working on something, you know, there's never anything I'm working on but what goes through my mind.

Lyn Hejinian of Berkeley's Tuumba Press, who published works by Rae Armantrout and Robert Grenier among the so-called Language Poets, speaks of the joy of sitting down of an evening to run a text document through Quark and massage the typography to her satisfaction. There's a fascinating discussion of the numerology you find in Larry Eigner (and the earlier concrete poets) where the monospacing of the typewriter creates a stoichedon layout. The point at which the line starts creates the precisely demarcated field of the poem. Hejinian: "Insisting that the fonts in which his work appears in books should conform to non-proportional spacing seems at risk of fetishizing something that wasn't particularly important." After Eigner's death Hejinian went to look at his manuscripts at Stanford: "It was all in typescripts and there was one page where he had laboriously noted where everything is supposed to line up. And then at the bottom he had typed 'I don't know, it's all an experiment anyway, and people will do what they want to do'. So you get a sense, but you don't have to be a curmudgeon about it. I mean, I feel that way about my own work when it gets published. If I care enough about the particulars of the poem's presentation, I have to do it myself. Which brings us back to the theme of self-publishing."

Schlesinger is a good listener and though he doesn't have an agenda he asks everyone about the distinction between book arts, artists books, fine press, and so on. Loney, the lone Antipodean, discusses the art versus craft aspects articulately and although I feel philosophers get too hung up in language and discussing the meaning of meaning – how the "word" becomes something "else" when you put quotes around it – I was pleased to note his critique of Derrida and Blanchot: "[they] seemed to know nothing at all about the history of the physical book over the last century nor anything of the formal properties of European and American contemporary poetry over the same period." This brings to mind sophomoric writers talking about deconstruction in the book form when they clearly never read *Tristram Shandy*. Ultimately Loney doesn't think the artists book has extended the notion of the "book" at all (quote marks his).

Mary Laird of Quelquefois Press tells how her travels inspire her art, but don't plan any trips with her: She barely survived a tornado in Wisconsin in 1984 and moved to California in time for the '89 earthquake. She talks about the patience required in setting type, and folding paper. "If Slow Food has made a comeback, let's watch those headlines for Slow Books!"

Jonathan Greene of Gnomon Press moved between the East and West Coast poetry scenes, knew Robin Blaser, Jack Spicer and Charles Olson, published Robert Duncan and learned from Graham Mackintosh but opted for the calm of Kentucky for his home where he got to know the consummate outsider publisher Jonathan Williams, printed his conversations with Bunting as *Descant on Rawthey's Madrigal* (1968) and designed his best-selling *White Trash Cooking* (1986).

Phil Gallo studied with Harry Duncan in Iowa City before establishing his Hermetic Press. He has strong opinions, and sounds like someone I would enjoy talking to, but would probably argue with: "I was writing a diatribe based on a lecture I gave and I submitted it to *Matrix*, but it was a little too polemical for them. John Randle said he wished he'd been at the lecture…" Decidedly the wrong venue! Gallo does a lot of printing for Granary Book of New York, run by Steven Clay. The latter talks about Jerome Rothenberg's influence, sending him back to the library to look at every book written by Robert Duncan, from the 40s, 50s, 60s, rather than just buying the collected works: "Going to the original sources and seeing the diversity of ways they were made, from the production to the distribution – I found it all fascinating. … Independent publishing and the kind of writing we're interested in, it's all of a piece. It's kind of unfair to lop off a hunk of writing for *The Collected Poems of Paul Blackburn*, and say, 'Hey, here's Blackburn.' That's really not the whole picture." He is also interested in how presses like Jargon of Jonathan Williams or Coracle of Simon Cutts find great work that is not part of the mainstream: "I think of the work of Thomas A. Clark and Laurie Clark, for example, which has found its place within the more radical side of publishing and writing communities, and publishing communities and readers – but why wasn't this work picked up by the Whittington Press? They lived in the Cotswolds for thirty years, they were just a few miles away from these people, but they seemed to have framed this pastoral, very charming word and image context into another field, and I'm really curious how they managed to do that. I was talking to Simon [Cutts] about it when we were out in Ireland, and he used this word 'refinement'. It's a different kind of refinement that they're getting at, and for that reason it just wouldn't show up on the radar screen of a press like Whittington. Whittington was doing very similar kinds of engravings, little drawings of moments and pastoral scenes with writing that may appear to be similar in tone to Clark's, but that's not the case at all."

While his business seems like a roaring success, Clay does have the usual cautionary tale. Thinking *The Book, Spiritual Instrument* by Jerome Rothenberg would be a best-seller they did it as a large-run trade book, expecting a reception "like the Americans liberating Baghdad or something, like we were going to be met with flowers, and hallelujahs! But in fact quite the opposite. There was some interest, but not really."

Charles Alexander of Chax Press, Arizona, was a student of Walter Hamady in Madison, Wisconsin, and felt the influence of his highly opinionated taste strongly, though there is a nice anecdote of a student telling Walter to shut up! Alexander also came to bookmaking

through Duncan, Ed Dorn and Robert Creeley. We also hear the familiar tale of academic feuds: Literature departments snubbing students from the Art side and vice versa. "No, this is for Art majors only!" Finally Alexander talks about the tactile quality of books and that is worth reading.

Then we "love with a love that was more than love" and get to walk on the wild side with Annabel Lee of Vehicle Editions, New York. Her thrilling story is one of the highlights of the book: she was working nonstop at Stonehill in the '70s, and then hitting the back room at Max's for the after party with the Warhol Factory crew. Drug dealers and Italian mafiosi surrounded her. She produced the lovely edition of Ted Berrigan's *Train Ride* (1971) but there are some nightmarish (& amusing) anecdotes connected to that too. (It is disappointing for Monotype to be continually lowercased in this book, along with other recurring typos.) But then there is this surprising voice of clarity amid the punk din of CBGBs: "I found the epigraph I chose for *Book Book* and it somehow seems even more apt now than it did then. It's a quote from Nicolas Barker from the 7 December 1973 issue of the *Times Literary Supplement*, an issue devoted to printing and book production. He wrote, 'Flexibility is the key to the future… the division between author and book-manufacturer will become fluid, rather than a watertight bulkhead. The division between professional and amateur printer will also become more fluid… If the lines between author and reader are less rigidly drawn with each party ready to accept a different division of work if the project demands it, then all will be well. It will also be, in theory, if not in practice, a return to pre-Gutenbergian methods of work.'"

After this intense interview the younger artists are a bit of a let-down, but Inge Bruggeman does elucidate one reality of the business of art: "By the time I finish a project I probably make 50 cents an hour!" She admires Gunnar Kaldewey's work where someone a few pages earlier excoriated him for his crappy "packaging" and inept typography (If there was an index it would be easy to look this up). OK, it was me.

Aaron Cohick muses on the strangeness of language. In fact any typesetter who sets his own work dwells on the peculiarities of word choices, orthography, letters, space, breath … so much passes in your brain in those moments between the type-case and the type-stick. "The first time I tried to set my own writing in lead type – it seemed dreadfully inadequate. Each word became too much of a presence and seemed wrong. The entire piece, once so close to me, was suddenly strange, an alien thing, heavy and glaring."

Scott Pierce of Effing Press (Austin, Texas) rounds out the collection. He also completes the circle back to the mid-century American poets with a trip to Bolinas and a young poet's rite of passage: "I smoked pot with Joanne Kyger, which is a milestone in my life." And then channelling some of the energy of the "Poetry Wars" of the 1980s he gives a reading in San Francisco which degenerates into a brawl where he ends up in a drunken fist fight with a friend of his: "We were both bruised and bloodied. We knocked the hell out of each other. It felt like we were rolling on the floor for hours. I was saying shit like, 'But I just published your book.' And he said, 'I love that book.' 'Why are you hitting me?' 'Because you're hitting me!' 'But I just wanted to help you.' 'I didn't need your help.' 'I thought you were gonna go after so and so.' 'I'm not here to fight.' 'Somebody threw a book at me. I thought it was you.'"

Lastly, who is still unaccounted for in this generation? Kickshaws definitely and Coach House Press of Toronto. Neither is "American" in the accepted sense: Coach House was established by Stan Bevington in Toronto in 1965 and is still running. Kickshaws, based in Paris, is a collaboration between British author John Crombie and American artist Sheila Bourne. They have produced over 150 of the most interesting book works of the past 40 years, in the *livres d'artiste* tradition. Despite these two omissions, Schlesinger's book fills in a solid piece of printing and publishing history, between the era of New Directions, Bern Porter and today. However, it has two flaws: there is no index (how many people talk about Robert Duncan, or Graham Mackintosh for that matter?) and the illustrations are blurry. The book is printed on off-white paper which is easy on the eyes but makes the photos indistinct and they are mostly small scale. A signature of coated paper with larger photos would have worked better. But the conversations are excellent.

There's a Poem I Love...

SOPHIE HANNAH

There's a Poem I Love...

There's a poem I love that cannot be found by Googling.
I've tried with the author's name, some key words, the title,
and there's nothing. This makes it feel absolutely vital
that I carry on looking. There must be someone who(gling)
at some point, on Wordpress, posted a verse or two(gling)
or a photographed page from a long-lost poetry recital.

There's a poem I love that cannot be found by Googling.
I remember the first two verses but not the last.
I've searched right back to my memory's distant past
in the hope of retrieving it all, but only a few(gling)
stanzas emerged. What on earth did we used to do(gling)
before we assumed we could find things super-fast?

There's a poem I love that cannot be found by Googling.
Wherever it lives these days, it is not online.
Should I put down my phone and go to the...? Nah, it's fine.
I'll write this new poem instead. There's too much to do(gling)
as it is – and there's Rightmove and Etsy, Deliveroo(gling),
and Instagram, Clubhouse and Facebook, Netflix, pink wine.

There's a poem I love that cannot be found by Googling.
I could ask folks on Slack. But, no, that won't flesh out the bones,
and they'll all be too busy doing more fun stuff on their phones.
They would only say 'Never heard of it. What and who(gling)?'
If I said it was written around 1952(gling)
they'd send the emoji that signifies heartfelt groans.

But it's such a great poem. The bit that my brain's recovered
is ace and the part I've forgotten was top-notch too.
Are you wondering how I know? All I know is: I do.
There were rosaries in the first verse, the word 'solar', and lovers,
And something about words repeated over and over.
(Let me know if this rings any bells. My DMs are open. Tweet 1 of 2)

Tweet 2 of 2

Also? Your loathed ex-friend, who comes to mind
Sometimes, or often? Google loves to find
People who share her name, but not her face.
(You spend hours peering closely, just in case.)

Indices

ANDREW HADFIELD

Dennis Duncan, *Index, A History of the: A Bookish Adventure* (Penguin) £20

I usually find reviewers who start off a review by writing about themselves insufferable and rarely get beyond the first paragraph. I am afraid, however, that Dennis Duncan's book has inspired me to indulge in a series of rather self-regarding reflections. Although there are many superficial differences between types of writers, in the final analysis there are fundamentally two sorts of authors: those who like doing indices and those who do not. The former group are decent and diligent souls who spend hours worrying that they have probably left out a stray reference to 'London' on p.27; that they may have not quite developed the proper range of pages dealing with an inchoate conceptual category such as 'Woolf, Virginia, thoughts about the future', and need to go back and include some earlier references, or even rethink the nature of divisions and sub-divisions in the draft index ('Woolf, Virginia, projections? fears?'); and they know that they will often wake up at night miserable and filled with self-loathing because their own haste and carelessness has deformed their otherwise lovely creation. The latter group simply find the index a bore and pay someone else to do it: in universities they send in unreasonable and selfish applications for vast sums to research committees then complain pompously that they are too important to have to waste their time on such trivia when the Rottweilers who have overseen the application turn their request down.

Reader, I confess, I was one of the second group. An early book (which shall remain nameless) has an index so lazily compiled and so incompetent that even I, its author, can find nothing within. However, I saw the light and became one of the chosen. For a later book (which shall also remain nameless) I compiled an index so meticulous and capacious that my publishers ordered me to reduce and trim some of the entries, an intervention that still makes me simultaneously proud and irritated several years later.

For anyone who has followed my path or thinks they should follow my path, or who is already one of the enlightened, there is now Dennis Duncan's engaging, learned and thoroughly enjoyable history of the highways and byways that constitute the history of the index. Dr Duncan does not confine himself simply to what we might think of as the modern index, but is really concerned with how information retrieval systems work to help readers navigate long works. His book relies on a variety of bookish skills in order to tell its story and close reading and literary analysis are as important as an overview of the history of the index *per se*. As he points out in a penetrating and entertaining analysis of *Pale Fire*, the index is an act of an author's generosity and imagination, putting themselves in the place of an ideal reader. What is a devious sleight of hand in Nabokov's story of a jealous and excessively interventionist editor annotating the poems of a recently deceased friend and rival, is that the index has to coincide with the plot. The author is in control of the narrative whereas, as Duncan points out, the index is really designed for the reader to make their own way through the text.

Duncan dates the birth of the index proper to the twelfth century, specifically to the need to negotiate the highways and byways of the Bible as universities were established to educate a literate priesthood able to spread the word of God effectively throughout Christendom. A retrospective acknowledgement of this moment in Western intellectual history, is the image of Hugh of St Cher, in the convent of San Nicolo in Treviso. Hugh, a Dominican, represented in his cardinal's hat and cloak, sits in a scriptorium, brows furrowed as he copies out a work. The image is important as the first portrait to show its subject wearing spectacles. It is an anachronism, as Duncan points out, because Hugh lived two decades too early to benefit from developments in optics that would have restored or improved his sight. Hugh's labours, alongside those of his energetic English counterparts, Stephen Langton (c.1150–1228) and Robert Grosseteste (1175?–1253), was instrumental in establishing the division of the Bible into chapters and verses so that it could be analysed by students, a key development in the history of the index. One of the welcome side effects of this new intellectual tool was glasses, an invention that has changed life for so many for so long (and, needless to say, without which this review could not have been written).

The origins of the index in Europe are intimately connected with the sermon, specifically, *aide-memoires*, or *distinctions*, written in manuals to provide a cleric with a handy list of subjects and information about them ready to instruct his congregation. For Duncan such expanded lists are 'evidence of a type of reading that might be thought of as indexical' (pp.67–8). The *distinctio* 'offers, not so much a map of the book, as the mind-map of a moment of creative reading' (p.68). Mighty intellectuals like Grosseteste were then able to develop the list, retrieval system, index, into a system that enabled a reader to navigate a book for their own purposes and order the material in their minds to suit their purposes. The index does not work as an undifferentiated list of words but has to grade the information in order to guide the reader and so enable them to make proper use of it. Soon the habit of reading in terms of remembering and reordering became commonplace and readers started to write their own annotations and lists in books, much as modern readers do, and which led

Flann O'Brien to imagine a book annotation service of various grades for readers who wished to appear learned without putting in the hours (the basic grade involved marks in the margins; the deluxe version had the annotator inserting 'c.f., Odyssey, 6.213', as well as tickets to European art galleries). The manicule, the finger in the margin pointing at a particular passage, started to appear in manuscripts and, later, early printed books.

There is an excellent chapter on the birth of the page number, another logical consequence of the development of the reading habits that Duncan describes. The first example is probably a sermon by Werner Rolevnick, later known for his chronicle of the world from its creation to 1481 (when 'the Ottoman Emperor Mehmet II went to hell for his wickedness against Christianity' (p.86)). Rolevnick's sermon was printed as a small book of twenty-four pages in Cologne in 1470 by Arnold Therhoernen, distinctive enough as an early printer to have had a font named after him in 2013. Duncan reproduces a picture of the opening page of the Latin sermon: half way down the right hand side is a numeral, looking like a 'J', the first page number. Before the page number became a standard book feature errors were made. A copy of Ranulph Higden's *Polychronicon*, written out by the scribe, John Lutton, literally reproduces another version so that a reference to Alexander the Great appears as leaf 72 when it should be leaf 66, a sign of direct copying from another manuscript that has been transferred here.

We are undoubtedly more used today to listening to complaints that digital retrieval systems and search engines promote careless and lazy reading as well as enabling users to retrieve massive amounts of disconnected information. These are nothing new and the early days of the index inspired the wrath of a number of ferociously erudite polymaths. Conrad Gessner (1516–65), physician, bibliographer, philosopher, natural historian, and so on, who packed an awful lot into his 49 years, recognized that the index was a good thing and ranked its importance only just behind that of Gutenberg's printing press. However, he was not entirely enthusiastic about its possible uses and cautioned against the 'wrong way to use an index':

Because of the carelessness of some who rely on the indexes… and who do not read the complete text of their authors in their proper order and methodically, the quality of those books is in no way being impaired, because the excellence and practicality of things will by no means be diminished or blamed because they have been misused by ignorant or dishonest men (pp.111–2).

Perhaps we can read this as a further example of the ways in which an index places the reader in control of the text so that we need to rely on a good, honourable reader to do justice to the material at his or her disposal.

Duncan not only conveys the excitement of scholarly pursuits and the pleasures of old works and manuscripts, but he has an excellent eye for anecdotes. A feud between two frenemies, William F. Buckley, Jr. (1925–2008) and Norman Mailer (1923–2007), led to Buckley

inscribing 'Hi!' in red ballpoint next to Mailer's name in the index of the copy of his book, *The Unmaking of a Mayor*, that he presented to Mailer, knowing that was where he would turn first of all. Sadly there is no record of what happened when Mailer opened the book and found the greeting. Indeed, jokes and amusing references are often inscribed in printed form. An academic book on tragicomedy has the entry, 'McDonald, M. I. 95, 187', not a reference to anything in the book, but the number of goals scored and appearances made by Malcolm 'Supermac' McDonald for Newcastle United before he signed for Arsenal in 1976. As the editor of *PN Review* informed me the index to Frederic Raphael's diaries, published by Carcanet, contains the entries 'Amis, Kingsley / Anus, Martin'. Other examples are too rude and personal to repeat.

The index, as the above example indicates, could be a battleground, as it was in the late seventeenth century. One notable and often hilarious conflict pitted the nobleman, Charles Boyle (1674–1731), a young academic of promise at Christ Church, Oxford, against the already established scholar, the king's librarian, Richard Bentley (1662–1742). Questions were asked about how much of Boyle's edition, *Epistles of Phalaris*, its editor had actually undertaken and rumours abounded that the star student had been helped out rather too much by his college tutors. After a barbed response from the pugilistic Bentley, in which he took to task Boyle's honesty and scholarly abilities, a lengthy anonymous response appeared, *Dr Bentley's Dissertations on the Epistles of Phalaris, and the Fables of Aesop, Examin'd*, better known by the more snappy title, *Boyle Against Bentley*. A central feature of the attack was 'A Short Account of Dr Bentley, By Way of Index', which contained entries for 'His egregious dulness', 'His Pedantry', and 'His familiar acquaintance with Books that he never saw'. The mock index had such an impact on later book culture that in the middle of the nineteenth century Thomas Babbington Macaulay, a well-known liberal, could demand that no damned Tory index his *History of England*. A variant was what Duncan terms the 'sarcastic index'. John Gay (1685–1732), author of *The Beggar's Opera*, noted wit and prominent member of the Scriblerian Club, was a leading exponent. His mock-heroic poem, *Trivia, or the Art of Walking the Streets of London* (1716), describes a group of apprentices playing football, one of whom manages to boot the ball through an upper sash window. The index has the entry, 'Glazier, his Skill at Foot-Ball', a sly reference that the reader needs to decode. Clearly the breakage was not an accident but a cunningly and perfectly executed scam.

There was also the 'weaponised index', invented by John Oldmixon (1673–1742). Oldmixon, a 'devoted propagandist for the Whig cause' (p.163) was employed by the publisher, Jacob Tonson (1655–1736) to produce the index for *The History of England* by Laurence Echard (c.1670–1730). While Oldmixon was an obscure and impoverished figure, later described by Alexander Pope as 'a virulent Party-writer for hire' (p.163), Echard was a pillar of the Tory establishment. Oldmixon, accordingly, took great pleasure in subverting his work by producing a naughty index. Where Echard describes the actions of

Richard Nelthorp, one of the Rye House conspirators plotting to assassinate Charles II, as treason, Oldmixon has the corresponding indexical entry, '*Nelthorp, Richard, a Lawyer hang'd without a Tryal in King James's Time*' (p.166). When James II finally produced an heir, rumours abounded among the Whig faction that a baby had been smuggled into her bed hidden inside a warming pan. While Echard describes the incident as an impossibility because even a relatively small baby could not be made to fit into a warming pan, Oldmixon provides the entry, 'Warming-pan, very useful to King *James*'s queen' (p.167), a masterpiece of po-faced disinformation. The entry led to a pamphlet refuting Oldmixon's sly suggestion, detailing the dimensions of the standard warming pan for readers who were unfamiliar with the common household object. As Duncan points out, this particular spat descends into 'a bathos that comes from the shift in tone from fury to wounded pedantry' (p.168). It was, however, Oldmixon's antics that Macaulay probably had in mind when he insisted that he could veto a hostile indexer.

Duncan is also good at showing his detective work. Shakespeare has Gertrude refer to the index in one of the more fraught scenes in *Hamlet* in which Hamlet confronts his mother with the consequences of her actions.

As he continues, getting ever more furious and confusing, the queen interjects, 'Ah me, what act, / That roars so loud and thunders in the index?' As Duncan points out, the line would appear to depend on the audience understanding that the index was often bound at the start of a volume as a sign of what was to come and only migrated to the back of the book some years later.

The book concludes with a spirited defence of the professional indexer. One has been compiled for this book by a member of the society for indexers, Paula Clarke Bain, and Duncan highlights the value of her good work by also including a sample of a computer-generated index (pp.303–7), which is, of course, unable to deal adequately with complicated categories and to distinguish pieces of information and place them under sub-headings.

The Index, A History of is a book that manages to be both enjoyable and informative, not least because of the author's enthusiasm for his subject. It also helps that he writes well, is a diligent researcher and bibliophile, and has a keen sense of what details work as stories, so the book will attract readers who are already fascinated by indexes and ones who do not yet know that, as a reader, this is a subject for them.

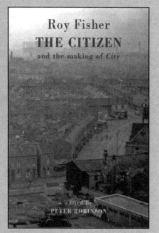

from Let Them Rest

SHERI BENNING

NE 36 19 23 W2nd

Two attic bedrooms, plaster and lathe, cotton candy pink, baby bird blue.
　　A wooden rocking chair, missing spindles. Torn-out
　　　　pages from *Little Red Riding Hood* –

　　　　　　　　　　　　　　hackles, incisors, the ravening wolf.

Master bedroom at the bottom of the stairwell. Dim. Cool. Lilac blooms
　　poke through the east window. Dust in the slant of late afternoon
　　　　light. Breathe deep. The smell of your mother

　when you were a girl and napped in the nest of her
　　　queen-sized bed. Beneath the metal frame and box spring,
　　　　a pair of calfskin leather baby shoes. Laces tied.

　　　　　　　　　　　　　　Do not touch anything –

　let her sleep. But sleep won't come to her eyes,
　　　Her right breast burns, mastitis, nipples cracked.
　　　　His arm heavy across her chest,
　　　　　soft *puh* of his slumber on her neck.

　All day the wolf at her back, stalks from room to room.
　　　What big eyes you have – the better to see.
　　　　What big ears. What big teeth.

　　　　　　　　　　　　　The better to tear inside,

　and hear what you cannot say –

　　　　　　　　　　　　　(all flesh is grass,
　　　　　　　　　the flower falls, bury the baby in lilac
　　　　　　　　　　branches. June blossoms,
　　　　　　　　　　　milk-soaked mouths).

　Upstairs, the children dream, lashes flicker,
　　　silver underside of poplar leaves. All day they pull
　　　　her dress, her legs, her arms, her hair, her sleeves.
　　　　　Let her sleep,

　but sleep won't come,
　　　the newborn in a basket by her bed,
　　　　her hand on the baby's belly to feel
　　　　　the small tide of breath

　　　　　　　　　　　　　(all flesh is grass,
　　　　　　　　　　the flower falls, lower the baby
　　　　　　　　into the well. Mineral drink of her spit and salt.
　　　　　　　　　She'd find her way back into your womb).

The wolf stalks room to room. Let her sleep,
but sleep won't come. Behind her eyelids,
the hatchlings who slipped
too soon between her thighs

(bird bones flensed,
a fine mobile, strung above her head,
quilled by moon).

Of

Rosalie née Tobin. Twenty-six, 1983.
She sits in her used LTD Ford Station wagon,
Co-op parking lot. Marriage on the rocks,

parents soon dead – lung cancer, heart attack.
July thunderstorm in the south sky. Supercells bloom
behind the hockey rink, the gutted stockyard.

Three kids under five buckled in the backseat.
She can feel their stare on her sunburned shoulders,
knows they know

she's crying again, so she cranks the radio.
Carly Simon. *Clouds in my coffee, clouds in my coffee.*
Full-throttle, off-key, eyes in the rearview, she sings

until the kids sing, too. Shift in atmospheric pressure
years later, and a vein bursts. Left front temporal lobe.
She falls on their farmhouse porch.

Florescent hum in the basement room off ICU.
Kids grown, a surgeon shows them scans –
blood rolls, cumulonimbus, *clouds in my coffee,*

and hail ricochets off asphalt, ozone and petrichor,
they're holding hands again, making a break
for the cold grocery store, wet-haired, shrieking.

Of

Amalia, neé Kobelsky. 1964.
Sisters Minnie and Beth on her front porch.
She hasn't seen them for more than thirty years

when at twenty she ran away from the farm
with the CP Rail section hand.
Before she draws breath,

a spaciousness, Beth's eyes the same
as rusted wheat, late autumn poplar leaves,
turned dirt, black currants, cold blades of frost.

The section hand was Protestant.
Might as well be dead,
last letter from her parents.

That night, her husband asleep, she steps out
onto their bungalow's back patio. New moon,
overcast, trapped light from the city horizon,

creek-bottom orange, when from the depthless
sky, the season's self-erasure,
the first heavy snow –

I don't know who she is.
I don't know who you're looking for,
she told her sisters as she closed the door.
Please go.

Ponteix, Saskatchewan: November 1919

Black blizzard, wet lungs,
snow, sand, cytokine storm.

A rope around her husband's
waist, tethered to their porch.

Someone had to do the milking.
Someone had to feed the horses.

Camphor, mustard, turpentine,
wormwood. Nuns in shadow-habits

plaster her chest. A rope around her
husband's waist so she could drag him back.

Farmers conscripted to dig frozen dirt,
plant tuberous corpses. Train cars,

coffins cracked, a whole threshing crew
found dead near Roleau, southwest of Regina.

Blue fingers. Blue lips. Cyanosis. By noon
the next day they buried her husband.

A rope around his waist so he could drag her
into his unmarked grave, rhizomes of men.

Nuns in shadow-habits beat her
with hailstone-fists to break up phlegm.

A neighbour found them in the nest,
the marriage bed, Johanna née Visser and

her mewling litter, her skinny baby birds.
She thought she heard the shadow

nuns whisper, *how will we divvy up
her daughters?* when she grabbed the knife,

the serrated blade, hacked and
hacked at the fraying rope.

Before

       their collagen hives dried
and her bones cracked, the richness
of her belly and thighs, grave wax.

Before bile and iron frayed
her best summer dress. Before
the cancer diagnosis, the heart attack.

Before the first winter she lived in sod,
dug-in to spear grass, wolf willow, aspen
roots, Arctic rose, whitetail scat,
slept in straw, drank snow.

Before weeks in steerage's salt
and heave. Before she said goodbye
to her mother in clouds of diesel steam,
the train platform in Mariupol.

Before Mother's letters stopped arriving.
Before fourteen babies opened her womb,
she was sixteen, 1890, a girl in Tiegenort,
holding her sister's hand in the still-

dark morning, processing through frozen
plum and pear trees, acacia hoarfrost canopy,
to church for *Maria Lichtmess.* Candlelit faces,
small moons, midway to equinox. Of

       Regina Elizabeth née Metlewsky –
the spill of her teeth in dirt, taper flames,
sparks of wheat, embers of burnt offerings.

Viaticum

Psalm 42

These things I remember: the light
  in crested wheat, spear grass, meadow brome,
    the pasture's first baize flush, late April.

When tears are my meat day and night:
  metal on metal echo in the farmyard,
    late afternoon. Oil-stained coveralls,

he's fixing tines on the heavy harrow
  while she sweeps grain bins for truckloads
    of bulk-seed – flax, barley, oats, peas –

sweet smell of last harvest's rotting crop.
  Sun low, barn cats grappling by the fuel tanks,
    air cooled by melting snow.

When they taunt, *where is your place?* the slough
  in the field west of our barns, stubble and dirt
    loosened from frost, furred willows,

frog chorus, the coyotes' dusk antiphonal,
  a bell's tongue in bone marrow. These things
    I remember as I pour out my soul.

Testament and other poems

KERRIN P. SHARPE

if you're looking for Leonard

today Leonard's expected
at Tower Hill station

the train arrives like a poem
with snow from Berlin
leaves from Manhattan

and in a darker version
twigs from the Feng trees of Shanghai
on its sooty roof

once Leonard appears
the platform becomes

both a place by the river
and a table of mercy

he doesn't make them angels
he doesn't make them lonely

   songs they sing together
   songs they never know

if you're looking for Leonard
just mention his name

he's holding the flame
for the Passover train

testament

I

a wedding party arrives
at the Cavendish
the wind lifts
blue moon rose petals
off a bride fragrant
with light blessed
at the Synagogue
testament to the Book
of Proverbs the Book
of Jeremiah
below the pier
a labrador already
frantic for the bride's bouquet
churns the mucky surf

II

a ghost train pinches
the jewelled octopus
swings her tin carts high
over the pier
fuses helter-skelter lights
side-kicks barrels of music
locks the jaws of clowns
spits at mechanical hares
jams the rifle range
the sea's persistent cough
shoots thick phlegm
into the jittery waves
six silver turbines
up to their necks in it

III

in the honeycomb of the pier
the homeless raise their voices
to fidgety angels
strung along the promenade
the light fades
Christmas drifts to sea
large parts not suitable
for over three's
pincers of plastic
claws of sticky oil
all those logs from where?
seagulls tumble
just as helpless
as the coastline

ice

a woman at the window
of a cabin in Norway
ice: an arm around a waist
a white wedding
the reindeer at her window
busking for breakfast blueberries
cloudberries ice: the reindeer's
eyes a groom learning to melt
the reindeer scattering
warm wishes of snow
the best man's speech
words that leave
a woman at the window
the ice more blue there

Pearl of Great Price

NICOLAS TREDELL

Marjorie Perloff, *Infrathin: A Study in Micropoetics* (University of Chicago Press) £20

The same is never the same is never the same. In Gertrude Stein's famous reiterative sentence, 'A rose is a rose is a rose,' the second 'rose' differs slightly from the first and the third 'rose' differs slightly from its two predecessors, visually, phonically, temporally and semantically. It is to this poetry (or poetry-in-prose) of minute differences that Marjorie Perloff's method of 'super-close reading' attends in this book: to the verbal, visual and sonic elements of a text, to 'the individual phoneme or letter as well as the larger semantic import'. Especially important here is the idea of the 'infrathin', the '*inframince*', a term that Perloff takes from Marcel Duchamp to indicate those slender, sometimes barely perceptible, nuances that differentiate near-identical experiences and subtly alter their meanings. Duchamp's examples include 'The warmth of a seat (which has just been left) is infrathin'; 'When the tobacco smoke smells also of the mouth which exhales it, the 2 orders marry by infrathin'; 'In time, the same object is not the same after a one-second interval'; 'The difference (dimensional) between two objects in a series (made from the same mold) is an infrathin one when the maximum (?) of precision is obtained'. Perloff contends that for Duchamp, and, by implication, for micropoetical reading, 'however minuscule the difference between one word or phrase or statement or another, the "difference", as Gertrude Stein puts it in *Tender Buttons*, "is spreading"'. Perloff contends that Stein's 'endlessly complex iterative prose' demonstrates this: 'the slightest repetition or shift in context changes the valence and meaning of any word or word group', as in the successive enunciations of 'A rose is a rose is a rose'.

In this perspective, the poet selects, and the reader attends to 'words and phrases with an eye' – and ear – alert for 'unexpected relationships – verbal, visual, sonic – that create a new construct and context' and generate 'infrathin possibilities'. While Perloff sees poetry as a vital corrective to clichéd generalization, she does venture to generalize about the possible nature of poetry: it 'might be defined as the art of the infrathin'. She is concerned, however, to differentiate the super-close reading that micropoetics entails from the close reading of New Criticism. The latter, she suggests, assumes that 'poetry is designed to convey a special meaning' and that poetic structure 'is always *semantic structure*'. It seeks to extricate a 'larger meaning [...] conveyed, in successful cases, by means of metaphor, irony, and paradox – the tropes of indirection'. In this respect, New Criticism always knows in advance, at least in general terms, what the 'larger meaning' of a poem that meets its criteria should be and the techniques by which it conveys that meaning. A similar point might be made about deconstruction and the notion of '*différence*', though in this book Perloff uses 'difference' in a Duchampian rather than Derridean

sense. In a deconstructive perspective, the ultimate meaning of any text is how it inevitably works to undermine the meanings it presents and to demonstrate that final meaning is always deferred – though certain poetic texts do this especially effectively. This affinity beneath the difference is perhaps partly why, despite pockets of resistance, deconstruction was able, for a time, to take over much of the American literary academy; it was a continuation of New Criticism by other means.

New Criticism, Perloff claims, virtually discounts 'rhythm, sound structure, visual patterning, etymology.' She acknowledges honourable exceptions: for instance, W.K. Wimsatt on Pope in *The Verbal Icon* and on 'the historical evolution of symbolic imagery from late eighteenth-century poets like William Bowles to Wordsworth'. But even in these New Critical readings, she asserts, 'sound structure and rhetorical device are always secondary, a given antithesis or chiasmus being designed to convey the particular verbal ambiguity that belongs to poetry'. This accounts, in Perloff's view, for the New Critical dismissal of William Carlos Williams, given his use of 'literal language, metonymy [rather than metaphor], and visual design', and of Pound's *Cantos* as, in R. P. Blackmur's words, a 'rag-bag'. New Criticism suppressed the 'radical difference' of the infrathin. For Perloff, the Russian Formalists offer a better grounding for micropoetics, combining the semantic, the phonic and the visual, even though, as she acknowledges, they never engaged critically with the 'new hybrid art forms of the twentieth century like the readymade, the installation, the "found" or appropriated poem'. But Perloff rejects formalism of any kind insofar as it entails neglect of context: 'A meaningful close reading cannot exist in the abstract, as it often did in the work of the New Critics and Russian Formalists.' It should be said, however, that she does not fully define what she means by context and that her contextual references, such as they are, often seem tacked on, inessential to the textual interpretation, and refer much more to the context created by other poets and poems than to social, cultural or political circumstances.

Perloff's micropoetical readings in this book have two aims: to show that such readings, in this case of specific Modernist works, 'can remind us what it is that makes poetry poetry' and to offer a 'revisionist history' of the poetry in those works, 'placing it in new contexts and suggesting unexpected alignments'. The first chapter examines 'the close verbal relationship between Duchamp and Gertrude Stein', contending that it is much closer than the more commonly canvassed Stein-Picasso link, while Chapter Two reads Eliot's *Little Gidding* 'as a brilliant verbal-visual-sonic complex'. The third chapter discusses Pound's 'spatial configuration, placement of words and ideograms, specific repetitions, and the larger design of a given page or set of pages,' and Chapter Four aims to attend more closely than most previous critics to 'the fabric of the language' of Wallace Stevens's poetry, 'especially the sound structures'. The fifth chapter focuses on Ashbery, one of Perloff's specialities, Chapter Six traces, in relation to Samuel Beckett's own poetry, his 'gradual transformation' from a 'critic of Yeatsian rhetoric' into an 'advocate of Yeats's poems', and the seventh and final chapter engages directly with Yeats's poetry.

A significant aspect of *Infrathin* is its construction of lines of descent for these poets. Perloff endows Eliot's *Four Quartets*, especially *Little Gidding*, with a particularly large progeny: its 'true heirs', though they might not have been wholly aware of it, 'were the new visually and sonically oriented poets of the postwar' and include 'American Objectivists' like Louis Zukofsky and Lorine Niedecker, and 'Concretists', from Ian Hamilton Finlay and Tom Raworth 'to such concretist-conceptual poets as Susan Howe and Craig Dworkin' who all, in their respective ways, replace 'the expressive first-person lyric' with 'an emphasis on the poetic *how*, experimenting with sound figures, visual constellations, paragrams, and etymologies' in order to stress 'the infrathin of poetry rather than its larger themes and topoi'. As for Pound, he is not only 'the precursor of the American Objectivists and Black Mountain Poets', but also 'paves the way for the great work of the Concrete poets' and enables the emergence of the later twentieth-century Brazilian concrete poets, particularly Haroldo de Campos. Wallace Stevens's 'Vacancy in the Park' is echoed and reinflected in the opening piece of Susan Howe's *The Quarry* (2015), 'Vagrancy in the Park', 'a hybrid text' that combines prose, poetry, 'formal analysis' and 'lyric fragment' in 'an homage to Stevens' that is also 'a foray into the new and different poetic world of the twenty-first century' and 'the lens' through which to see Steven's late work as complexification rather than diminishment. Ashbery's 'genuine heirs' are less 'the tribe of John' than, say, 'the unlikely "language" poetry of Charles Bernstein and Rae Armantrout'. Yeats, in poems such as 'The Wild Swans at Coole,' might be seen as 'a precursor of later sound poets', though she feels that 'he would not have understood – or approved of – the term'. Perloff's proposed lineages are often, in good Russian Formalist fashion, provocatively defamiliarizing and they are also, to a certain extent, heuristic, enabling the discovery of unexpected elements in both begetters and heirs. The concern to make links to concrete and language poetry can sometimes seem a little hobby-horsical but Perloff is too balanced and informed to tip over into obsession and eccentricity.

It is Eliot above all whose poetic prescience Perloff praises: she affirms that his 'great gift' was 'to use the very smallest particles of language – letters, syllables, paragrams, etymological puzzles – to point the way toward a new poetry' that 'could counter the endless clichés and platitudes broadcast by the media in the age of mechanical reproducibility and later in the digital age'. This idea of poetry as a counterweight and challenge to inert uses of language is a key component of Modernist poetics and criticism, and perhaps, by now,

an over-familiar one that itself risks becoming a cliché and platitude. There is also, however, a contradictory element in Perloff's staging of a contest between poetry and 'mechanical reproducibility', and this emerges in her plaudits for both Eliot and Pound's embracement of the typewriter. As she observes, 'the look of poetry *on the page* (or the screen) has changed completely, thanks to the typewriter in the early twentieth century and the computer a few decades later'. The phrase 'thanks to' implies that these forms of 'mechanical reproducibility', rather than being detrimental to poetry, helped, as per Pound's famous imperative, to 'make it new', and she casts both Eliot and Pound as techno-aesthetic prophets. Eliot perceived that 'the new poetry of the twentieth century, now composed on the typewriter to be both seen and heard, must pay attention to each and every letter, syllable, and word in a given poem' and Pound understood 'that the typewriter offered possibilities that made the "traditional stanza", a print block surrounded by white space, seem constrictive' and opened up innovatory potentials that came to fruition in the digital era. 'Poundian page design' prefigured the current capacity to deploy, via a personal computer, '[t]ypeface, font, layout, color' and 'visual image'.

Perloff's readings, closely attentive to spatial, phonic, temporal and semantic features and to the absence or displacement of the 'expressive first-person lyric', offer many aperçus and acute summations. She is, characteristically, very good on Ashbery, although she implicitly acknowledges that he presents a challenge, in key respects, to the kind of microcriticism she is advocating insofar as his poetry is of a kind 'whose verbivocovisual temperature is intentionally low' – in other words, not that much to see here, at least with microcritical spectacles. His poetry does, however, eschew the coherent first-person 'I', seamless continuity and true connectives, even though, as Perloff points out, it foregrounds false ones – '*and*, *but*, *if*, *though*, *when*, *now*, *yet*, *so*, *still*, *nearly*, *after*, *which*, *so that*, *what if*, and especially *as* – as in "As we know", or "If this is the way it is"'. In Ashbery's 'Variant', for instance, '[s]peech is not so much heard as overheard, with the reader in the position of someone, say, on a train or at the next table, trying to make sense of the bits and pieces of other people's conversation'. In this and similar poems, '[e]very phrase [...] sounds just familiar enough to recall something else, and yet the collocation of narrative fragments and meditational bits is entirely Ashbery's own'.

In Bernstein's poems, as in Ashbery's, 'words pop up in surprising slots' but the 'discourse radius' of the two poets differs: while the senior poet's lines 'are charged [...] with erotic double entendre', Bernstein's are loaded 'with allusions to money, to business practices and capitalist exploitation'. Rae Armantrout's 'use of ellipsis and the silence of white space is radical', prompting the reader 'to fill in many blanks in order to make any sense at all of her abrupt abstractions'. Beckett's 'they come' 'avoids the first-person pronoun entirely, presenting the poem's statement as impersonally and anonymously as if we were looking at the procession of figures on a Greek vase' – and although Perloff does not say this, her Keatsian allusion cues the observation that Beckett's poem is less an 'Ode on a Grecian Urn' than an 'Ode as a Grecian Urn', albeit a minimalist one.

Perloff completed *Infrathin* as an octogenarian in a time of pestilence and political turmoil, and in September 2021 she turned 90. In its concision, clarity and insight, her latest book compares favourably with the bloviations of her near-contemporary, the late Harold Bloom, in his posthumous *Take Arms Against a Sea of Trouble*s (reviewed *PNR 258*), where the slivers of gold must be dredged from the depths of a vast slough of senescence. But this comparison should not be taken to imply that Perloff's latest book is good 'for her age'; it would be a good book for a critic of any age. It bears the hallmarks of *echt* criticism; it makes you want to read or reread the texts it discusses and to apply the micropoetical method it outlines to those and other texts, while not being bound by it – and Perloff shows the way here, departing from strict methodological adherence when the insights demand it. As she herself puts it, literary criticism 'will never be an exact science', and ultimately, as T.S. Eliot once observed, 'there is no method except to be very intelligent' – which of course Perloff is. If her fondness for paronomasia may permit a pun on her surname, she is, as a critic, a pearl of great price who shines like a good deed in a naughty world.

To Vladimir Nabokov

FREDERIC RAPHAEL

Cher Maître,

Today, when every tease and tout writes "Hi, Fred", Shelley's antique courtesies retain their call on me. My father recommended that, if in doubt, call a man "Sir", never a woman "madam" (despite Macaulay's famous first words). Born in the same year as yourself, named in honour of Little Lord Fauntleroy, Cedric had been a world amateur champion tango dancer. His dago turn served him better than small talk. When it came to the ladies, he offered me no advice save Spinoza's *caute,* rubberised. I discovered much later that he had failed to honour it; hence the appearance, in middle age, hers more middle than mine, of my half-sister Sheila, no Augusta Leigh. I never heard my father say "fuck", with or without a screamer, my wife's early term for an exclamation mark. In *Speak, Memory,* you recall your father saying – fifteen-years-old were you? – "You threaded that girl?" Neither reproach nor praise, was it? A *constatation.* Lightly flossed shins did she have? Life is one story; story another life.

I associate getting little things right with those sketches, in one of your critical compendia, of the disposition of seats in the old Russian railways. You say, in *Speak, Memory,* that you received a "college blue" for tennis while at Trinity, Cambridge, in the 1920s. I have never heard of anyone else being honoured in those terms but hesitate to cross words with a man whose vigilance entailed several sub-species of *lepidoptera* being tagged *Nabokovensis.* When you posted nature's oldest law as being "the survival of the weakest", you saluted the catch-me-if-you-can't specimens that eluded your prehensile passes. Divide through by motive, ignore excuses, withhold explanations, is that the lesson of mastery? In your books, caressing the details delivers the art of the matter. Branding Fyodor Dostoyevksy a "journalist", you diagnosed him as a case of scribbler's rush. You conceded that his manic tendencies came of having been subjected to mock execution by the Tzarist authorities, but in your aesthetics, sympathy procures no remission. Then think of Raskalnikov. Genius, *quand-même,* Fyodor?

In the smart New York crowd into which, thanks to Bunny Wilson, you came to be translated, who else was heard to mutter that the Romanovs' don't-do-it-again mock execution of Decembrists was a cruel, all but mere, parody of ruthlessness compared with Communism's murder of millions of innocent citizens? *Invitation to a Beheading,* the Red Queen's speciality, put your loop around the smirk that Bertie Russell observed on Lenin's face when, in power, he gloated over what Auden was besotted enough to call "the necessary murder" before he had Christian second thoughts. Osip Mandelstam alone of those within Stalin's grasp scorned him, recklessly, as a black beetle.

Enough of the Georgian poet still lodged in Josef Vissarionovich's Kremlin for him to ironise at Boris Pasternak's hedging – as good as ditching – when quizzed about the suddenly toxic Osip. After listening to a spasm of vicar-of-Braying, Stalin said "Is that the best you can do for your friend?" He then ordered that Mandelstam be left untouched, for a while. Did you ever have a good word to say for *Doctor Zhivago,* Paster/nark's swank apology for want of outspokenness when it might have cost him dear? Nobel Prizes too can hang around a man's neck. You, we may guess, were never a contender. Irony rarely strikes gold. Who last heard a Swede laugh?

You always insisted that Russia's *ancien régime* never descended to the mass transports of the slaughterer at the centre of our wartime pin-up trinity; cigarette, pipe, cigar their fuming markers. Was close reading ever more dandily validated than in your prognosis that the Soviet State would disintegrate because the Russian language was bound to get its own back against the *apparat* that degraded it into New Speak? The English journalist Bernard Levin is the only other scribe I remember to have diagnosed the Soviet Union as bound to disintegrate.

As you pointed out, Levin is an odd name for Tolstoy's conjugally virtuous alter ego in *Anna Karenina.* Can it be that Levin's indexed proximity to Lev – as Tolstoy was liable to be addressed – deafened the Master to the Jewish ring of Levin? Do any Jewish characters feature in Tolstoy's work? You advertised no ear for music, he no nose for Jews. Bernard Levin lacked *Solus Rex* dandyism, but you and he fought the good fight, albeit ("all bite" an English M. Jourdain called it) *separatim.* Bernard's prose alone was handsome. Who ever wrote more studiedly on water? Most western intellectuals, few with wider experience of the Soviet State than Potemkin-style tours afforded them, hedged their bets and softened their buts, Orwell and Malcolm Muggeridge excepted. You pouched your words as David that quintet of smooth stones before slinging Goliath.

The conceit that jumped Vladimir Nabokov into the world's literary limelight was, *bien entendu*, *Lolita.* You had already shone, locally, in 1920s Berlin. In the *émigré* press, those reduced to the rancorous were treated to literary caviar. Sirin's salted tales were stuck on the great ass of Soviet pretensions. As for the Viennese witch-doctor, scorn for Sigmund's Oedipal schematics certified your unambiguous love for your father, shot by a Kremlin hireling whose target Vladimir Dmitrievich, true gentleman, shielded with his person. I remember reporting to you how Leon Trotsky, in his *History of the Russian Revolution,* spoke of your father as the most intelligent of the Kadets. I am not sure how welcome you took his compliment to be.

When did you start to teach yourself the English which garnished your first stories enough to appeal to *The New Yorker's* Bunny Wilson? There was an English Bunny, whom you never knew, I think: Bloomsbury's David "Bunny" Garnett. I went to see the author of *Aspects of Love* when he was eighty-six. Separated from his wife, Angelica, he was living *tout seul* in a cottage with an earth floor in the Lot-et-Garonne. He had first seen Angelica Bell in her cot. He looked at the pretty infant (and her mother Vanessa) and said "I shall marry her one day"; and so he did. Who denounced Bunny Bunny as a double-dyed wanton, except for the bride whose freedom he had filched? Many years and three daughters later, she divorced him. *Aspects of Love* was one of the first books I ever reviewed; for all Bunny Garnett's erotic experiences (Tiresian and buy-sexual) he made mishmashed potatoes of them all.

You had only your recherché wits to live on when you and Véra first landed in N.Y.C. I see you in that tight rented bathroom, brown suitcase for knees-up desk, translating yourself into a professorial author, Pnin and ink, his what-the-Dickens English with implications more arcane than natives were liable to decypher. Destitution never dented your *superbe. C*omedy, with a twist, followed whatever befell you. Making America yours (as Kafka did Amerika, though he never went there), you chose to be more amused than affronted by Roman Jakobson's casting-out vote when rejected for an Ivy League literary professorship. Reminded that you were a remarkable writer, he is said to have said, "One might as well appoint an elephant professor of biology" or words of that tusky order. While you found a niche at Cornell, you disdained to put down roots. You and Véra bowled from one sabbatical absentee's house to another. I imagine you, like Max Beerbohm's H.J. sniffing ranged shoes outside bedroom doors in the *Trois Couronnes* at Vevey, nosey for traces apt for fictional appropriation.

Had it not been for Graham Greene, *Lolita* might never have crossed the Channel, then the Atlantic, from its lodging, alongside other, naughty, books published by Maurice Girodias in his Traveller's Library, apt to be read one-handed, as J.-J. Rousseau had it. Those commas enclosing "naughty" exempt me from implying that you supplied a catch-penny contribution to the pornography amongst which you were softly shelved. Hard-backing came after you extracted yourself from that blue Parisian range. Greene furnished you with a ticket to the *via dollarosa* which wound up leading to the Grand Hotel, Montreux, whither I was seconded to find you.

Time was that any number of hot books, in English, were on sale in Paris. They were liable to confiscation if found among the luggage of returning Anglo-Saxons. Back in 1929 Chicago, my mother Irene (silent latter "e") took pride in parading down State Street reading about James Joyce's Cunty Kate, assuming she got that far (how many do?). Her copy of *Ulysses* (odd/issues concealed within) was smuggled in from Paris by Buddy Cadison, one of her *beaux,* after he had visited Sylvia Beach's Shakespeare and Company. In the second lustrum of the 1950s, some of my Cambridge contemporaries made a louche secret of contributing erectile material, *Thongs* among them, to Girodias' Travellers' Library. I scanned them in the *Librairie La Hune*, in the Boulevard St Germain, adjacent to the *Café de Flore* where during the war Sartre and the Beaver hogged the stove. Not so *braves Crillons,* their camp fieriness parodied the resistance Albert Camus and friends were actively pursuing on the *chemins de la liberté*.

During the Occupation, Sartre took artful care that his play *Les Mouches* passed the Nazi censors. It opened on the Right Bank, to an audience of le tout Paris *collabo,* on D-Day 1944. Only after the Germans had departed did he come out in valiant style, against France's capitalist liberators, as de Gaulle soon did against the same allies, entitled in his case "Anglo-Saxons". Has anyone construed the plague of flies in Sartre's play as being not so much the occupying Fridolins as the seething Jews? How else did it pass the German censors? It's no great surprise that Sartre's *copain* Camus came to be shot down, in *Les Temps Modernes,* as a phoney *philosophe*; what was insupportable for Sartre and his go-get-him marksman, François Jeanson, was that Camus had been *engagé* when it was a matter of life or death, not a politic flourish.

Did Graham Greene light on *Lolita* while cruising at *La Hune's* wide, slightly tilted display table or did some specialist pusher mark his card? G.G. relished the mackintoshed anonymity he impersonated in Louis Malle's *La Nuit Américaine.* I remember, when at Cambridge, hearing that he was known as "Grim Grin" *chez les*

Français amongst whom he later tax-exiled himself. Greene's Catholicism, whatever its origin (was he not seeking to bed, if need be wed, some rich American R.C. beauty?), seemed to offer access to the dark side of life, quite as Willie Maugham's medical degree had to the back streets of Lambeth where his Liza languished. The success of *The Third Man* may have derived more from Carol Reed's movie (and Orson Welles' sinister gleam and beat-that Swiss roll on the Prater's Big Wheel) than from the intrinsic merits of Greene's sketchy novel. Did you ever mutter an admiring word about him?

While they toyed at privileged access to hellish depths (Scobie's the deepest, in *The Heart of the Matter*), Greene's "novels" were calculated, no less deliberately than his "entertainments", to excite but never shock. He hinted at impropriety, treason too, as luridly as the market might relish. Faith unfaithful went but so far. Grim greenery was his trade. You, I recall, took pride in the colourful alphabet in your cerebral font. G.G. played at being something finer than a commercial author but never risked confounding his public. Catholicism was his wubber wing, as childish swimmers have been known to say. Has anyone yet undertaken a profile of the divinity as depicted by post-Auschwitz English writers? T.S. Eliot and Greene are conspicuous in advertising His abiding salvationary powers. *The Family Reunion* and *The Living Room* bore witness that, for the right people, He had survived the Holocaust and remained at the receipt of custom.

More naughty schoolboy than Byronic wanton, Greene's choice of *Lolita* as a book of the year – 1956, was it? – applauded a recklessness he never emulated. His terrestrial father was a housemaster at a minor public school where Greene himself was a pupil. While his characters flirted with damnation, their author was wary of exciting a bad report at home. His cheekiest excess came when, as grub street film reviewer in the 1930s, he made play with the idea that Shirley Temple's cute little girl was a Hollywood prototype of your little Lo. The good ship Lollypop might have featured the pair of them as part of its welcome on board. The damages it had to pay for Greene's upskirting of Shirley T. bankrupted the publication he wrote for, but her innocence was never retrieved. That plug for *Lolita* was in line with G.G.'s paying habit of tickling the nonconformist conscience. Wilful, prolific anonymity as he had been in Weimaresque Berlin, Vladimir Nabokov was suddenly a hotshot *in propria persona*.

Kingsley Amis, still a young man but scarcely angry, stood in an *alt*-English corner at the time that Greene put you in his Christmas box. The author of *Lucky Jim* was at the peak of reprint-on-reprint fame. Victor Gollancz had hesitated to publish Orwell's *Animal Farm* and *1984,* but what danger was there of Kingsley ruffling important feathers? Oxonian iconoclast, alongside the soon to be waning Wain, young Amis was no champion of Beowulf nor yet of Leavis's po-faced Great Tradition nor, when yetting on, of experimental innovation. He came to exemplify the post-Suez style of aggressive modesty. Making a diet of hands that fed him, he accepted a Somerset Maugham Travel bursary and wrote *I Like It Here* by way of a no thank you letter.

The old *New Yorker* rubric "No Fine Writing Please" could have furnished a badge for The Movement Kingsley consorted with. Its wry writers and viceless versifiers embodied the neo-brutalism of Utility Furniture. Commercial and critical, Kingley's early work Yoricked at the expense of the literary tradition dodo plumage had served to dignify. I happened recently on a jaundiced cutting from *The Daily Telegraph* in which, at the end of a slew of novels, *Lucky Jim* is seen off, by some double-deckered Julian, as of small and perishable wit. I had listened on my bulky-batteried portable radio as Jim Dixon cut up his host's cigarette-burnt sheets, harbinger of the *anarithmon gelasma* of England's protracted self-destruction. Was sat/ire ever more aptly sub-sectioned than in Kingsley's I'm-all-right-jacketed fiction?

You were, no doubt, promptly alerted to the repel-boarders tone of the Amis review of *Lolita.* Larry Durrell used to say that if an author was deep in some remote jungle, his best friend would make sure that a runner came toting bad reviews in a forked stick. Kingsley switched, with ease, from being Jim Dixon to a critical Dixon of Dock Green (no, I do not at all expect you to take the dated reference). With Jack Warner's black and white TV copper's cry of "Oy, what do you think you're doing?", Kingers nicked Humbert Humbert fair and very square. What conforms more self-righteously than the non-conformist conscience? *Lolita* as *Alice in Wonderland* in erotic travesty shocked the family-man that Kingsley impersonated before Jane Howard tripped in to play the wicked witch of the Cheltenham Festival.

Why deny that you came out as the sublime Reverend Charles Dodgson never did? That *Lolita* should also ring changes on the shamelessness of the old hot book has to have been part of the Petronian fun of writing it. Did you ever claim, as addled admirers reported, that the adventures of little Lo satirised your initiation in the U.S. of A.? Such spurious insights announced their chefs to be the very type of foot-notaries you satirise in *Pale Fire.* When did you claim that *Lolita* was not scandalous, Humbert not a humbug? What Movement could ever have welcomed you as a member? Promising that second-rate was as good as it was prudent to be on the tight little island, Kingsley won many English prizes. One example is enough to prove that your imagination composed on a scale beyond his. No, not *Laughter in the Dark.* I am thinking of that simple short story, set in an alley of trees in the Luxembourg Gardens, in which a couple are having a tart-tongued, gesticulating quarrel when one or other realises that, at the far end of nature's archway, a green child is watching and listening. The couple sense that they are fouling his memory with ugliness. Do they kiss?

In the autumn of 1970, I was commissioned by Columbia Pictures to go to Montreux to convene with you (and converge with handsome producer John Van Eyssen) to discuss writing a movie script from your latest, tubby novel, *Ada.* Stanley Kubrick's movie of *Lolita,* with the incomparable James Mason, had been little more than a *succès d'estime,* but your fame remained such that, *Ada* still in proof, not yet a pudding, you were able to have Hollywood studios send their plenipotentiaries to the Grand Hotel Montreux. Seated in the big, quiet main reception room, they were handed advance copies and invited to consider their verdicts and the zeros attached to them. Only bids sealed there and then would be entertained. What hospitable device was ever more exacting? No one was obliged to make a bid, but each delegate dreaded missing the Big One and the reproaches of his studio if another turned it into a hit. Now or never paid a sweet dividend: something of the order of a quarter of a million dollars was promised before the Byronic prize was taken home to L.A. and laid before its new owners. Victory proved sweeter than its fruits. On unexcited studio reading, *Ada* was no naughty chick nor did her story promise golden eggs; no Humbert hummed.

The Sixties and my Oscar had made me well-off and the brief darling of the biz. My 1960s fee had, however, like that of anyone on the A-list, collapsed with the market. Luckily, we had nice houses, here and there. I was happy to take my winnings and revert to writing fiction. A copy of my latest, *Like Men Betrayed,* was in the boot of my Cambridge blue Mercedes 280SE as I delivered Beetle and the children to Bordeaux airport for their flights back to England and, we presumed, the right schools. No deal had yet been struck for me to write a screenplay of *Ada,* even for a slump price, but I was promised fat expenses for my excursion *en Suisse.*

My selection as putative screenwriter was explained by my Oscar and, no doubt, capped by my parodic eulogy of *Ada* in *The Sunday Times.* Unlike the producers, I appeared to have some idea of what it was all about, Byron's daughter Ada (inventor of a prototypical computer) in particular. The Columbia brass needed someone whose ingenuity would justify the price they had paid for the rights. I had relished the wit of your remake of a miscreant world, but I had no prompt sense of a movie shambling towards Montreux to be born. Had it not been for the lure of meeting you, I should, as bridge players used to say, have passed in sleep.

Beetle's flight was in the late afternoon. I was instantly lonelier than fancy had proposed. With Flaubert's warrant, I scanned the whores, some transvestites, no doubt, as they stilted themselves on steep heels on the *trottoirs* around the glass-bracketed market in the centre of Bordeaux. Then, in conscience's custody, I made for the big bookshop where I furnished myself with *un peu de lecture,* Vidal-Naquet and company; Greek scholarship made appetising in the French style. I happened on a copy of the *Tri-Quarterly* which included a segment on your work by whoever they were.

Armed for head-down solitude, I went, with none but a timekeeper's appetite, to a modest, stiff-chaired restaurant where I remembered there was a *table d'hôte.* Salesmen and other solitaries traded the small change of their quotidian pursuits. There was only one female in the company. Neither girl nor yet middle-aged, *bien poitrinée,* she was eating modestly before repairing to wherever it was that she danced other people's nights away. She had worked, for however long and when, in L.A. Our conversation was spiced with insiderishness. Before she got up to go, she told me, with no manifest flirtatiousness, where she was strutting her stuff; last show one in the morning. As soon as she had gone, one of the other men at the table said, *"Vous auriez dû la suivre, monsieur. Vous aviez des fortes chances."*

I walked back to my respectable hotel. The next morn-

ing I set off to drive across the Massif Central to Lyon. Stranger in my own car, parcel and chauffeur, I cannot remember stopping for lunch. As evening drew its October drapes, I made for Beetle's and my favourite one-star Michelin restaurant, at *Les Halles,* a one-street village in the loopy hills ahead of Lyon. Perhaps Monsieur and Madame Rigaud would recognise that I still was who I had been. Shutters closed, pinched light outlined their exclusivity. How could they do that to me? The lonely man takes the world personally.

I drove down towards Lyon, fat, cold city. Too late for a restaurant, I stopped at a *voyageurs* hotel on the far side of a humpbacked bridge in a sorry suburb with a handsome name. After she had shown me to a room, I asked the landlady whether there was anything to eat. How should the scene be shot to convey what failed to happen? Did she watch me peel her apple? Was I detaining her with my small talk or was she loitering? Neither young nor old, she seemed at home with her solitude as I was not with mine. Nothing took its time. No, she did not stay. No, I did not want her to.

My sleep changed gear as the *poids lourds* did, catarrhally, as they got over the humped bridge. It was Sunday morning. I was not due to see you (and John Van Eyssen, our delegated producer) until lunchtime on Monday. Fettered in freedom, I chauffeured myself to the bank of the Saône and parked outside the three-starred Restaurant Paul Bocuse, where Beetle and I had lunched a few times. Seated one file from the windows looking over the river, between two hooped families, I pretended to be hungry. How long I seemed to wait for my *moules marinières*! I instructed myself to take note of the conversation between two businessmen adjacent across the aisle. The writer had better be an eavesdropper, a spy, a voyeur, a double-dealer, had that been not your theme more often that once? I lent so much ear to the two men that I put my fingers in the sauce where the *moules* were basking, not the fingerbowl. *"T'as-vu ce type qui se baignait les doigts dans la sauce?"* Do you know the story of Duff Cooper, when put down as *"espèce d'objet de valeur"* by a Parisian taxi-driver, responding saying, *"Écoutez le Belge?"*? I lacked the ambassadorial gall to give it weight.

No, inspector Javert, I cannot remember what I did for the rest of that day, nor where I stayed the night, in France or *Suisse.* My next sighting of myself is at the Château de Chillon, Montreux's sentinel, stone toes sandalled in Lake Leman, on Monday morning. I shivered where Bonnivard was chained for nine years before Byron and Percy Bysshe stopped by to underline his fame. For all my pious dawdle, I was early for lunch at the Grand Hotel. I settled on a blanched bench to revise the *Tri-Quarterly* until it was time to go in and register. John van Eyssen had not arrived. I was soon being shown into a room no wider than a single-car garage. Its terrace had space only for an upright, armless, metal chair. There was a shower, not a bath; and no bath towel. *Ah les bons Suisses!*

Memory cuts to a round table on the glassed terrace at the right front of the hotel. My strip of memory has you and Véra and me being served with veal and vegetables. Did we have something to start? Did we drink wine? It was not long before you found occasion to accuse me of being fond of anagrams. I recalled John Fowles' snaffled phrase "I denied the soft impeachment". Nevertheless, as people rarely say but often write, you scribbled a Russified jumble, ending in -ski, on a paper napkin (can it have been? At the Grand Hotel, Montreux?) and turned it to me. "Do you recognise the author?" I had the wit to look from you to Véra, implacable examiners both, and then, but a calculated tick or two from immediately, I swivelled the paper back and said, "Kingsley Amis, isn't it?" Matching my beats, as your admirer Stanley Kubrick would put it, you said "This is a very interesting young man."

I said, "Is it interesting to be well prepared? I can still rehearse the main provisions of the Sullan constitution if that will get me anywhere; no future in being a tribune of the plebs, you may remember." I listened to myself without pride but with a certain amusement as I played your bowling. No, I cannot remember much else that was said at that blanched table. Did we have cheese? If so, it too was blanched. As you left to have a rest upstairs, you warned me that you were going to take another look at my review of *Ada*. Did you imagine you might find some unexploded squibs *là-dedans*?

The lunch may have been an audition; I had no expectation of a scholarship to follow. My interest in the matter was meeting you. Usually, I can reproduce something of the vocabulary and accent of memorable personalities. I am sure you delivered excellent English, with a where-did-that-come-from timbre, but you seem to have retained the patent. You were courteous, you agreed to be amused as you allowed me to clear the hurdles you set, but no voice comes back to me, only the Cheshire smile.

I may have flattered you with an account of the duration of my motorised pilgrimage to Montreux. Perhaps that evoked your account of travelling to some upstate New York university in mid-winter to deliver a consignment of vintage arcana. The professor deputed to welcome you had a prompt confession: owing to some sorry maladdress, your lecture had not been signalled in the college press. He led you into the wide lecture room that you would, no doubt, have overflowed and more today. With an apologetic hand, he waved at the dozen students he had managed to cull. "A choice company," he said, "and, you will notice, nicely distributed in the available space." That had been then, now – as Véra was prompt to say – you filled halls to overflowing, when you cared to favour them. She, it seemed, was company enough for you and your imagination.

When John Van Eyssen arrived, flushed with frustration at having been late for lunch, I reverted to being the kind of scribe who is supposed to save the sum of things for pay. *Ada* was a fat version of that tricky paper you swivelled to me, challenge to which I had no prior riposte. I did have one good idea, which I produced as if it were an example of copiousness to come: my opening shot was of the White House, seen at ground level. The camera would then tilt and widen to include the flagpole on the roof topped by the Union Jack is seen in proprietorial mode. This chimed sweetly with the parallel world, without internal combustion engines or portraits of George Washington, in which you set your

incestuous romance. Do I remember flying sleighs, somehow propelled by super-horsepower, or is that my *père Noel* confection? You listened to my busking with indulgence, saying at some point "This man is like a good doctor. Whenever anything seems a serious problem, he promises that it can be taken care of."

Quack as I might, I was quite sure, by the time the fair Van Eyssen took me out to a handsome dinner, that no ingenuity of mine, however neatly dressed, would ever induce cash-strapped Columbia to, as they used to say, divvy up. When I paraded my wit, it was in the hope of no better reward than your conniving slope of a smile. We were there, Van Eyssen and I, in tribute to your gambitry in extracting all those dollars by means of a sublime bluff. At some point on that next morning, you and I were armchaired in one of the grand reception rooms in which I cannot recall seeing a single other guest. Sharing the knowledge that neither of us spelt out, that we had conned Columbia without the least dishonesty, we talked of other things.

You told me, in particular, about the explosive rupture you had had, quite recently, with your one-time sponsor Bunny Wilson. His review of your labour of patriotic love, the translation of *Eugen Onegin* which you affected to pass for a superbly groomed pony (your term), had something in common with Sartre's procured panning of Camus: revenge for a quality beyond the critic's competence, except to deface. The effrontery with which he challenged your command of Russian put rouge on his cheek. Exile was said to have tarnished your vocabulary. In particular Wilon ridiculed your translation, as "Kinkajou", of some native Russian beast Pushkin had laired in his text. There was, I suspected and did not say, at least some justice in ridiculing the translation of a small tree-happy mammal, unique to Central and South America, to the Siberian veldt (let's say) where it was never seen to swing. Were you teasing? Even your alleged howler had to be something like a *hapax legomenon*.

I was conscious, oh God yes, of not having been invited to your apartment. I could make no secret of my commercial motive, but liked to presume that there was now something father-and-sunny in our dialogue. Certainly, we were close enough for you to tell me how, when you done rallying with him, Bunny W. sent you a Christmas-time envelope from which, in lieu of a card, a black butterfly flopped. The attached note told you that its author had "never enjoyed a literary duel as much" as your altercation when Pushkin came to Shovekin. You looked at me in telling silence. I should be cheating if I claimed that your eyes grew lustrous or your throat thicker. You did pause. Then you said, "I did not enjoy it in the least". That rare moment put the capper on our encounter. Oddly, we did not talk about *Pale Fire,* a masterpiece I enjoyed much more than *Ada*. Mary McCarthy, the 20th century's Madame de Villeparisis, judged *Pale Fire* a masterpiece, not wrongly but also, surely, to ladle derision on Bunny Wilson, her overripe ex-husband, by implying that he had a defective ear for genius. Her calculated folly in marrying him excited no self-mockery in Hannah Arendt's New York oppo. No more, we might go on, was Arendt ever likely to have seen herself as fortune's fool when she became Heidegger's virginal doxy. There is no end of paper loops in the Great Chain of Being.

I left you a copy of *Like Men Betrayed,* as apt, title-wise, a tribute as I could offer. I must have driven away, fast, before lunch, but memory's tape flutters on empty. Did I hope that I might have a line from you about my novel? Perhaps you were never much of a correspondent. We have yet to see your Collected Letters, if such a collection can be made. Spontaneity was rarely your style, was it? You always wanted to have the questions ahead of any interview, I seem to remember; so too did Heidegger. I recall the story of how you challenged the philosopher Max Black to a game of chess when you were first his colleague at Cornell. He beat you quickly the first time, after which, in polite style, he offered a return game, won almost as swiftly. Is it true that you never again played competitive chess, but established unchallenged mastery in devising problems of diabolical ingenuity? You must have told the story yourself, which is excuse enough, I hope, for recalling it. Did Ingres ever play in an orchestra?

A year or two after you and I failed to tire the sun with talking, Beetle and I drove through Montreux on our devious way to Italy. I halted outside the Grand Hotel, but feared embarrassment, yours or mine, if I claimed acquaintance. It had been no surprise that nothing came, then or later, of the project to make a movie of *Ada.* Despite that publishing scoundrel who bloated some antique flirtation of yours into something all but adulterous, you and Véra seem to have been content, never contentious, whether in that bathroom study in N.Y.C. or in the sequestered luxury of the Grand Hotel. Did you ever own a motorcar? I see you either on foot, silent and reticulate, or helping yourself, and Véra, to a car and driver.

There is always a detail that the keenest researcher's diligence cannot caress. For small instance, one summer's day almost ten years after our meetings, I was called from the tennis court adjacent to our French house to take a call from the Canadian Broadcasting System. Some guy, in Toronto was it?, thought I should want to know that you had left us. I thanked him for the courtesy but wondered why he had bothered to call me. He said that Véra had told him that, of all the writers you had known, you had had the keenest sense of rapport with me. So? So damn.

Mes hommages, cher Volodya, si j'ose dire. Frederic.

He Rises and other poems

AMY CRUTCHFIELD

Yew

When I think of yew,
I think of those berries
the colour of a glacé cherry
or apples dipped in candy.
The colour of the knave
of hearts who takes the trick,
the colour of bets we placed, and the losses
gamblers chase.

The colour of a woman's lips in rouge absolu.
They say we paint our mouths this way
to make them look more like
the box for a defibrillator. Stop me
and start me up again.

The colour of a nosebleed on tissue
or exsanguination, which is red
but also blue. The colour of a heart on fire
like the one Augustine holds high
in *Veritas* by de Champaigne.

One day each of us learns,
or doesn't, about the circles.
Circle of pleasure, circle of sustenance,
and where they intersect, a lens,
sweet as it is slender.

Yew berries are a pseudofruit
(and all of science proves it).
Fruit found false because it is not born
from the female part transformed.
Would we manage life with language
we would call these berries, arils. Beloved
of thrush and waxwing; bright and plump and
wildly toxic.

In the painting by de Champaigne
Augustine sits at his desk beside the window.
He holds his rosy *cor* aloft
as beams of truth ignite it.

So much flame might mean epiphany,
though insights aren't always that graphic.
Sometimes one ember,
a single wind-borne word, will settle.
The house burns down the same.

When I think of yew
I think of the summer I became one.
I stood in La Haye-de-Routot,
with a hollow inside my trunk
so big they stuck a door on it
and made the chapel of St Anne.
Non sum qualis eram, I am not
as I once was.

When I think of yew
I think of all the deaths we die,
now so few,
where once were many.
And of girls lying wan and lonely,
white robes and sliver'd posies.

When Idad's boughs are bowed unto the ground
bowed so low they brush the earth, new roots shoot,
take hold somehow.

Truth or fire – what comes first?
In his painting de Champaigne seems sure.
Truth sets the fire burning. But is it that clear?
Could not fire set truth? The soul a pyrophyte,
the banksia mind cracked wide.

He Rises

after Lawrence and Boruch

from the chamber, pale and grand and naked.
His penis is missing, and yet, I see it,
frail and awry, beneath a cloud of hair.
His breast and the pillar of his belly glow
for a Kandelaber burns inside him too
though all is softer, all is smoother.
Ambiguity, round-faced, persists. His lips,
sit slightly open, as if to let
desire escape like breath.
His gaze is lifted, distant. Only longing is left,
pellets of it, in the hollow of him. Recall
his box of sycamore, seven strings of gut,
ten fingers still tender, one dark centre.
Right hip cocked, left leg crossed, heel raised so
that his toes rest lightly on the earth,
he leans sharply into space, toward a support
now lost. Who stood beside him?
Was Pothos borne by Love, our ally of the night,
Epistrophia? There is no place I do not see you.

Pothos II

Museo Centrale Montemartini

By lips slightly open, and eyes
a little sunken, we might recognise him.
This is the work of Skopas, and this figure,
rescued from misnomer, is no Apollo
but Pothos – god of longing.
Among the dead, he breathes, exhales desire -
which moves in waves toward its object.
And what did Skopas know of this moment, this motion,
arriving footsore and dusty in Megara,
his chisels in a roll of leather?
Did he catch it in a calm pool of water,
or watch it pass, as the shadow of a cloud across the plain
face of an apprentice
in the workshops at the growing temple?
What had he learned of longing and its
fierce metamorphosis.
For the categories are not fixed,
needs jostle on the ladder, and we
do not sleep, we do not eat.

Pothos III

The stem moves at its own pace, leans as each
toward their solace, on sticky countertops
in laneway bars,
or the beaded gardens of Mo'orea,
in the bruised light
of the understory
Epipremnum aureum
tenders itself
toward that brightness -
silver vine,
marble queen,
hunter's robe,
Ceylon creeper
and because
it can survive
in darkness,
Pothos is
Devil's
ivy.

Latin American Sonnets

LEO BOIX

A Latin American Sonnet

There is a palm tree somewhere, and a bird
of paradise that speaks to me in my dreams.
Well, not actually a bird, more like a blurred
vision of a plane crossing the endless seams
of a continent too big to fit here, in this isle
of gold where we plant elder for shade, sit
under a dusty sun, whatever it takes. Miles
away from everywhere, in my dreams a Brit
asks all the questions, and I often reply: who-
ever comes for tea will one day have to leave
for a better world. I end up kissing the beau
who is from here, or just about, so naive!
A blue parrot repeats my name in old English,
I wake up. Phew. It was a dream, well...*ish.*

A Latin American Sonnet II

We were all Latin Americans, *todos latinoamericanos,*
in that tiny rickety newsroom on the Holloway Road.
The boss, a Colombian like Tony from The Sopranos,
the chief editor, a Chilean émigré who often exploded.
The accounts were done by a Mexican lady called Paz,
who never swore and could speak Nahuatl and Mixtec.
Once a month a Bolivian came to check the old Macs,
and then there was *moi,* a young Argentine at his desk.
The paper obviously called Noticias Latin America.
Some said it was run by cocaine lords, a Latin mafia,
some complained we were too lefty and anti-American.
We worked listening to salsa while eating fried tilapia.

A Latin American Sonnet III

We are the only Latin Americans in Deal;
there was a loud Uruguayan lady who left
for Madrid and was never seen again. I feel
like a parakeet sometimes, I have to confess.
I have a boyfriend now who, like me, came
from Buenos Aires, he has lived here almost
all his life, people can't tell 'til he says his name.
Our old house is a pseudo-Argentine outpost
where to drink hot maté, eat steaks, inside here
we speak an odd Spanish, a mismatch melee
of words we've created: *mono-pato, adormir,*
as if we were in our own world, both castaways.
Lets drink to that and to our long life together,
sometimes is tough and sometimes it gets better.

Zoom View and other poems

MARTIN HAYDEN

On Not Coinciding

Say there's one moment in each lifetime
when it's granted to us to see each other
as we are: when was it? I think of
latish on a wet day, in Alligin Shuas,
weather clearing, we've all set out

to walk to Diabaig, even found
the start of the path easily for once,
and you're five or six, in your small boots
(it's far too far and strenuous
for you really): you're exclaiming

to me about the puddles, and
as if you've just then discovered
how to do it, jumping from stone
to stone with the perfect balance
of one fully attuned...

Or that last evening, before your five weeks'
disappearance (which became forever),
when we'd clarified preparations

for the morrow and its trials –
did we touch hands, an almost high-five,

me seated, you standing there, looking
warmly into me for one moment?
What *was* that? I came to think,
a longing for a hug which I missed
(it is now *my* longing and grows stronger).

But perhaps it was a clear-sighted
all-perceiving farewell...the moment
passes...as we say...and no-one
knows the truth of it now, except
that our significant perceptions

rarely coincide: we've moved on
before we know we've missed something
precious, and looking back
we're not quite sure what it was,
or even if it would be good to know.

Early September Dusk

Early September dusk, I'd sat as I like to,
the study window with curtains open,
the blue in the sky going down, but something
persisting long after the solid black
there'd be if you put the light on.

Fuchsia, myrtle, privet hedge, and the path
from the front gate through them, and you
sidling in, of course, the check in your movement
as you see me, your grin of surprise....
I construct that again, as I've done
a hundred times, at first when it was possible,
though when it happened it was winter,
the curtains were closed, I didn't know.

You say I've written this poem already,
I'm better off out between the trees
watching for a star or a bat, with the moths,
or with Montale and Alberti, those connoisseurs
of the dark, their words a trawl of spirits.
My timid handline comes up empty,
just a winking aircraft, a late starling –
until a light switch finishes it all.

(Quaker Meeting)

We're all settled, silent, twenty-five boxes
with twenty-four faces and one mug of tea,
when I notice past the screen on the piano stool
Vasko Popa's *Collected Poems* (Anvil)
drooping slightly over *Noces*, 'les essais
par Albert Camus', both half-balanced over
an admittedly solid Penguin George Fox
but not quite centred on an Edmund Rubbra
Concerto for Piano and Orchestra in G
(miniature score) and *PN Review*s
in a six-deep warp over one *North*.

So, as, between the silence, from one box
a bell chimes in France, from another

off-screen water rushes into a bowl,
I contemplate the fulcrum, the gravity,
the possible shift in momentum, the gulf
into which Popa and Camus might tumble,
a seething snake-pit of twenty-first century
cable, for wi fi disc, laptop, USB,

and opposite, on top of the old cabinet
bought in New Zealand, still heavy
with now unplayed LPs, a dual language
Dante's *Inferno* with, on the cover,
from the Baptistery in Florence, like a pike
in a Ted Hughes poem, the devil
with a half-swallowed human in his mouth.

Meter, Feelings, Knowing

a conversation with Nigel Fabb

MARK DOW

Nigel Fabb is Professor of Literary Linguistics at the University of Strathclyde in Glasgow. His books include *What is Poetry: Language and Memory in the Poems of the World* (Cambridge 2015); with Morris Halle, *Meter in Poetry: a New Theory* (Cambridge 2008); *Language and literary structure: the linguistic analysis of form in verse and narrative* (Cambridge 2002); and *Linguistics and Literature* (Blackwell 1997).

This conversation was conducted via email in May/ June 2021.

MD: Your essay 'Why is Verse Poetry?' appeared in the September 2008 PN Review, *and we first got in touch after I wrote a letter to the editor about your comments in it on the 'tip-of-the-tongue' phenomenon, so let's start there. The 'tip-of-the-tongue' phenomenon interests you, I think, because it's an example of linguistic structure detaching itself from 'content'. It points to the existence of 'unnameable' or 'unspeakable' content. On a larger scale, this feeling of knowing something we cannot put into words is what has been labelled 'the sublime'. If my summary is more or less accurate, can you lay out the milestones of your interest in these topics?*

NF: The tip-of-the-tongue feeling is a feeling relating to knowledge, and one of a number of 'epistemic feelings' which belong on what William James called the fringe of

consciousness. It is related to the 'feeling of knowing', identified by J. T. Hart in 1965, which involves a feeling that we know the answer to a question, but cannot yet express it (but are eventually able to). I have just completed a book for Anthem Press, *Thrills, sublime, epiphany: how literature surprises us,* and which is about what (following Alf Gabrielsson) I call 'strong experiences'. These include experiences of suddenly feeling that we know something very important, as in the experience of the sublime and of 'epiphany' in all its variations. Sometimes – as in aha-moments and some epiphanies – it is possible to put that knowledge into words. And sometimes it is not. I suggest that all of these experiences begin with surprise, when we perceive something which we cannot quite fit into what we already know; and already in that, there is the possibility that what we perceive cannot be put into words, since we only have words for what we already know. There are all sorts of reasons why we cannot put into words what we think we know, and there are psychological explanations for these. Raffman's *Language, Music and Mind* explores various sources of ineffability, and Sperber's *On Anthropological Knowledge* shows how we can fail to understand our own beliefs, including very profound beliefs, which would make them ineffable.

For your 2013 MIT lecture 'The Metrical Line', you timed the pauses at the ends of lines in readings of 54 poems –

including Dylan Thomas reading Milton – and used this data to discuss 'line boundaries'. My students often want to be told the 'right way' to handle line breaks when reading aloud. I tell them there's no 'right' way, but that in an Ammons poem, for example, you wouldn't pause so much as to make the sense/syntax impossible to follow. Then I found audio of Ammons himself reading the short poem we'd been discussing, and he reads it in just the way I had assured students no one would, pausing at the line boundary for a startling amount of time. And Creeley, I gather, was interested in just that kind of disruption of his syntax to emphasize his line. What are your thoughts on these 'performances' or approaches?

It's a style of performance, neither right nor wrong in principle (in my view). Pausing at the end of lines is maybe a way of emphasising enjambments when they happen, so there could be a good aesthetic reason for doing that. It also makes the metrical form and indeed other aspects of the poetic form more clear, since they are dependent on lineation. Poetic form is always an addition to linguistic form, and so some level of mismatch is always potentially there. I think in fact that poetic form makes literary language less language-like, and this discrepancy produces low-level aesthetic feelings.

What do you mean by 'less language-like'?

Language has various kinds of form, including lexical (vocabulary), syntactic (sentence structure), phonological (speech sounds), and prosodic (grouping of words into spoken units). Poetic form adds lines which are another kind of form, and metre and rhyme, which are also additional, even though they refer to linguistic form; the addition of these forms means that literary language is not quite like ordinary language anymore. Plus, the words and phrases can be reordered or omitted in ways not found in ordinary language. In my *PN Review* article, I argued that there is some reason to think that literary language might resemble language, rather than just being language.

You're interested in metre at its micro-level – degrees of stress, how long it takes to read a pentameter line, how long one pauses at line 'boundaries'. At a different level, as you were just explaining, you're interested in the 'ineffable' and in how poems surprise us. You're interested in the physiological processes and how they connect to or even cause our aesthetic responses – such as the physical arousal that seems to underlie our experience of the 'ineffable', or the cognitive processes that account for our sense or feeling of closure (in a poem). Are you trying to connect the measurable with the unmeasurable, the way mathematics is the basis of music and, presumably, of music's effect on us?

At least one kind of ineffability emerges from the micro-levels, in the sense that we have perceptions which are too fine-grained for us to have words for them; Raffman calls this 'nuance ineffability'. The relation between mathematics and music's effect on us might be because we have cognitive abilities which respond to the mathe-

matical forms underlying music; but also because we have statistical or probabilistic knowledge (which thus has a mathematical basis). That probabilistic knowledge is involved in forming expectations which can be violated or met, which is a source of feeling.

Donald Davie, in his essay 'Syntax as Music' on Susanne Langer, says that most poets who say poetry is like music don't really know music. He writes: 'In [Langer's] view a poem is like a piece of music in that it articulates itself; and in thus establishing internal relations, establishes also relations of feelings, building up the structure, the morphology of feeling, and telling us "what it feels like to feel"'.

This might be a way of saying that the meaning of the poem arises from the combination of the parts, which when taken apart do not have the same meaning (i.e., the opposite of Brecht, 'pluck a rose and every petal is beautiful'). This is true in principle for any utterance, which can always be more than the combined meaning of the parts; this is because language is partial evidence for meaning rather than fully encoding meaning. The same must be true for the non-meaning effects such as 'feelings'. But incidentally that means that even the text as a whole is not enough, but must always be contextualized to produce meaning. Consider the strong experiences: Stephen gets an epiphany from the clock but his friend Cranly does not (in Joyce's *Stephen Hero*) because of many contextual factors, personal factors, cultural factors etc. It's not just the clock, any more than it can be just the poem, which produces the experience. Also, a lot of these strong experiences come from fragments, not from whole texts – Housman can't shave because his hair stands up when a line of Keats strays into his mind, not the whole poem – and surely this is 'feeling'.

CHOMSKY, STRESS, TIME
You mentioned in an email that your title 'Linguistics of Surprise' is an homage to Noam Chomsky, who supervised your thesis at MIT in 1984. Can you explain the allusion and also say something about the relationship between your project and Chomsky's?

The allusion is to Chomsky's book *The Minimalist Program* which ends with this sentence: 'We are left with hard and challenging problems of a new order of depth, and prospects for a theory of language with properties that are quite surprising'. It is very beautiful in its understatement, and an example of the poetic quality of some of Chomsky's writing. Morris Halle (Chomsky's long colleague) and I finish our book *Metre in Poetry* (2008) with 'We conclude with R. Shammai that much work remains to be done'. Last sentences are fun. My first co-written book, *Literary Studies in Action*, with Alan Durant, ended with our phone number, in case anyone wanted to call us.

Here are two connections to what I learned from Chomsky and more generally at MIT. First, my project is about knowledge: the feeling of suddenly knowing something significant. Chomsky's fundamental concern is with knowledge – in his case knowledge of language, which he argued was not like knowledge of other things; this is clear from his first book *Syntactic Structures* (1957) on. The second connection is the idea, also in *Syntactic Structures*, that simple component parts combine to produce very complex outcomes; so in my current book I try to use only some relatively simple notions already present in standard psychology and from them build an account of these rare and special experiences. In a way this goes back to the Davie quote – the idea of emergence of complexity from a combination of simple parts.

Did you or Durant get any phone calls from readers?

Two people called us. This was all before e-mail of course.

Do you write poems?

No. The closest I've come to making poems happen is that I commissioned poems in different languages from Gwyneth Lewis, Meg Bateman and Drew Milne for the covers of *Journal of Linguistics* 50th volume.

Many readers of PNR *are probably interested in prosody but might not know the linguist's angle on it. I myself have tried and failed more than once at reading Halle and Keyser's* English Stress: Its Form, Its Growth, and Its Role in Verse *(1971). I apologize for this question, but can you give us a lay explanation of 'generative metrics', of which Halle is considered the founder, and of the gist of your book with him?*

A generative theory is a set of instructions for building something. A generative metrical theory is a set of instructions for building a scansion, which is a particular kind of complex structure, and that scansion is fitted to the line of poetry in a way which is also governed by instructions or rules. Each distinct metre has its own set of instructions. Simple version: the instructions for iambic pentameter end up by building a scansion which has ten metrical positions, alternating weak (odd numbered) and strong (even numbered). The line of poetry is fitted to the scansion, according to specific rules: the basic rules for this metre are that each syllable must fit a metrical position, which means that there are ten syllables in the line, and syllables carrying fixed stress must not match to weak positions (so for example, position 5 is weak and we would not expect a stressed syllable in this position in this metre). If the scansion can be built and fits the line, then the line is metrical, and if not it is unmetrical (both relative to iambic pentameter, in this case). There are further complications, for example sometimes two adjacent syllables can fit into one metrical position as in synaloepha, and sometimes there is a final extra unmatched syllable, and the rhythmic constraint is also subject to some variation. The purpose of a generative metrics is to understand exactly what in our ordinary linguistic capabilities gets adapted to produce the modified kinds of language found in poetry, so it is part of the general linguistic project. It isn't about interpretation, and in that it is very different from a literary account of metre.

There are some big differences between this and standard foot-based approaches to metre, of the kind more commonly found in literary analysis, in which for example the iambic pentameter line is made of a sequence of five iambic feet, and feet can be substituted for other feet. In generative metres, the line is always taken as a whole, not as a sequence of conjoined and separable feet. And a really crucial point is that the metre and the rhythm are not the same, but can have quite a loose connection as indeed they do in iambic pentameter, where every line in a poem can be in the same metre but every line can have a different rhythm. This is because the metre is not altered to fit the rhythm of the line by for example substituting feet, and this is because the metre is assumed to under-determine the rhythm: that is, only some aspects of the rhythm are controlled by the metre. One knock-on effect of this is that the standard literary practice of saying 'a spondee is used here with this meaning' won't work, because there is no spondee. Generative metrics is much more holistic, rather ironically, than the standard approach; again, the generative approach looks to me something more like what Davie wanted, seeing it as a whole, not a combination of parts.

The Fabb and Halle book presents a particular theory of metre which is supposed to account for both English and the major metrical traditions of the world, many of which we discuss. We take the view that in metrical poetry, the most important factor is that the line is fixed in length, with permitted variations: that is, a metre is basically a counting system, so that iambic pentameter lines are counted out to have ten syllables. And if the metrical poem also has a rhythm, the rhythm is dependent on how the metrical elements are counted, which is always a counting by pairs or by triplets, which emerges as a rhythmic pattern.

Does 'no rhythm' mean lacking a patterned repetition of accent or stress?

Or of syllable weight or tone type, yes. Most of the traditional Celtic prosodies have syllable counting but no regular pattern of accents. French alexandrines control stress only very minimally. The North Indian *arya* metre groups syllabic units (*matra*) into sequences but doesn't pattern stress or weight. Japanese poetry counts syllabic units but does not have rhythm. Metre doesn't always have rhythm but it always has counting.

Define stress.

Stress is a property of a syllable, and it is a psychological effect, not an acoustic one. We judge the stress of a syllable in context, relative to adjacent syllables. So stress is always relational, and not an inherent property of the syllable; Mark Liberman's demonstration of that was an important innovation. Various acoustic properties can indicate that a syllable is stressed, such as if it is loud, or high, or long, or several of these together. In words of more than one syllable, the stress pattern is determined by the generative rules by the relational mechanisms just noted, and is stable in the sense that you know where the stress is, it can be listed in a dictionary etc., and incidentally these fixed stresses in multisyllabic words are the stresses which are hardest to put into weak metrical positions in poetry. One of the interesting things about stress in English and many other languages is that it is determined by counting syllables backwards from the end of the word. It is a good example of how our knowledge of language is atemporal, because structure can be generated backwards.

What's the shortest possible explanation you can give for the fact that stress has been a fundamental aspect of verse form in English, assuming you agree that that's the case?

I don't have an explanation, and it puzzles me. Why can't English verse more frequently use syllable counting with either no or limited control over rhythm, like the French alexandrine? Or, to take another possibility, English syllables can be differentiated like Latin or Greek into heavy and light, and indeed syllabic stress is determined inside English words relative to syllable weight, but English has few poems in a quantitative metre and even they tend to use stress as well. Perhaps it is just the dominant influence of some very major writers who wrote using stress-based metres. Or there may be something about English sound structure which determines it, and some generative metrists do make these kinds of proposal about the relation between languages and metres.

Years ago in the Berryville Old Book Shop, in Berryville, Virginia, I found a reprint of an intriguing book, A Study of Metre *by Thomas Stewart Omond (1903). Is this a book prosodists or linguists take seriously today? What do you think of Omond's effort to replace the 'crudity and dubiety of scansion by syllables' with 'scansion by time-spaces'?*

I cannot think of anyone referring to it. There is a long-standing tradition of arguing that metre is organized relative to time, but no generative metrists argue for it; metres have declarative or map-like properties and not procedural or directional properties. In contrast, songs are organized relative to time, and you can see the difference between the atemporal poetic metre and the temporal musical metre when you see how variable the ways are of putting the two together in a song based on a metrical poem. Incidentally, in the Fabb and Halle theory we argue that iambic scansions are constructed backwards across the line, from end to beginning (while trochaic ones are constructed forwards), which shows again that at least in our theory metre is completely outside time. Perhaps metrical poetry gains an aesthetic because metre is an atemporal structure which is matched to the temporal structure of speech in real time.

FROST, GOD, WORDSWORTH
Which languages do you speak/read? And where were you born and raised?

English, ok with French and German. I co-wrote a grammar of the Sudanic language Ma'di, with Mairi Blackings, now Professor of Literary Linguistics in Juba, which he spoke but I never learned, and so I contributed the theoretical linguistic expertise required to work out what the forms of the language were. Born in England, brought up in Dylan Thomas's 'ugly, lovely town'.

You've said (also in an email), 'I assume that thought is entirely linguistic', as per Jerry Fodor, that 'thoughts are sentences in the head.' How do you account for, say, Temple Grandin's Thinking in Pictures?

Thought isn't entirely linguistic. Some of it is, and when it is linguistic it has some interesting properties which may not be available to nonlinguistic thought. For example thoughts in a linguistic form make it possible to have thoughts we do not understand. I suspect also that ineffability only arises because of the possibility of linguistic thought.

Can you give an example of having a thought you do not understand?

Any belief (which is a kind of thought) which I cannot fully explain will do. If I was religious, then it would be some of my religious beliefs, probably (cf. Dan Sperber again). But for me, perhaps the belief 'that there is something strange about narrative'. I can talk around that, and indeed have written about it; but I don't feel I fully understand that thought, even though it feels true to me: an example of a feeling of ineffable significance.

Back to ineffability. This is Robert Frost: 'Make no mistake about the tones of speech I mean. They are the same yesterday, today, and forever. They were before words were – if anything was before anything else. They have merely entrenched themselves in words. No one invents new tones of voice. So many and no more belong to the human throat, just as so many runs and quavers belong to the throat of the cat-bird, so many to the chickadee. The imagination is no more than their summoner – the imagination of the ear'*. This sounds almost kabbalistic to me – not what I've ever associated with Frost. And I came across it soon after something that surprised me in your own article on 'profound ineffability': 'Ineffability is content without structure... [T]his way of modelling how a concept might be ineffable fits with some of the theories of the ineffable, in particular the idea that God is an (ineffable) Word, but a word which is not part of a language and cannot be compared with any other'. From this follow 'verbal taboos such as a prohibition on speaking the name of God'. And I'll add that some religious Jews would not write (in English) 'God' but 'G-d'. What are you getting at when you write 'Word' with the upper-case W? And what thoughts do you have on the Frost comment?

No specific meaning meant by Word, but I want to mention Joann Sfar's comic book *The Rabbi's Cat* in which the talking cat is punished for violating the prohibition. Naming is interesting when it comes to ineffability, because names are almost not words at all, because they have no generic meaning, just placeholders for bits of reality. That's probably why they are dangerous to say or write. I like Frost's quote – it goes back to what I said before about combining a limited set of simple things into something complex; and it's like Chomsky's notion that language makes infinite use of finite resources, which is what he means by 'creativity'.

Are you religious? Were you brought up in any religious tradition?

No.

Your article on ineffability opens with Wordsworth's Prelude. *Let's end with Wordsworth here. This is editor Jack Stillinger's note to 'Nuns fret not…': 'In November 1802 Wordsworth told a correspondent that the music of Milton's sonnets "has an energetic and varied flow of sound crowding into narrow room more of the combined effect of rhyme and blank verse than can be done by any other kind of verse that I know of"'. What do your investigations tell you about what Wordsworth is saying here?*

I can't answer this because I don't know Milton's sonnets well enough to know what Wordsworth meant. The only connection I've drawn between them in my work is in an article on 'OF in *Paradise Lost* as evidence for the metrical line'. I show that Milton uses 'of' not only at the beginning of the first two lines, but more frequently than one might expect at the beginnings of lines in the poem (27% of all instances of OF are in the first of the ten metrical positions, and 5% of all the lines begin with OF, making it the second most frequent line-initial word). And you can see Milton's influence on 'Tintern Abbey' in which OF is used at the beginning of 23 lines. 14% of all the lines begin with OF, and in a possible echo of *PL*, it initiates the second line of the poem. That's not answering your question, but it tells us something about what Wordsworth liked in Milton, I suppose.

What would you like to know about language that you don't know?

I'd like to know whether poetic or literary language produces any kind of distinct epistemic feeling or arousal, in itself, just from its difference from ordinary language. This is a view which to some extent reflects the traditional notion of 'tension' as a characteristic of aesthetic language and aesthetic objects more generally, but it's a notion which is very difficult to test. I'd also like to know why in Ma'di it is not possible to end a past tense sentence on an object, for example why the translation of 'I read the book' is not a possible sentence but 'I read the book yesterday' or 'I read the book for sure' are both possible. It's been puzzling me for almost 20 years, and I once pointed out to a group of bilingual Ma'di and English speakers that you could say it in English and not in Ma'di, and they completely agreed while saying that – as for many of the facts about our own language – they had never noticed; they knew it without knowing it. I have not been able to find a good specific linguistic explanation for this, as a linguist should.

*Quoted in Christopher Benfey's 'The Storm Over Robert Frost', a review of Mark Richardson, ed., *Collected Prose of Robert Frost*, in *New York Review of Books*, 12/4/08.

Chaunt

JOHN ROBERT LEE

'Time has no future'
Toni Morrison

1.
arrange your griefs
with white roses
wreaths & yellow lilies —

her grace, elusive
penetrating gaze, untranslatable
smile at her lips' corners—

the purple balloon rises
above scraping trowels, hymns
appealing for remembrance, an unplanned tear
running off the cheek of a drizzling sky.

2.
on this first afternoon of your last April
sadness plays the fool
as news of your death sounds
like knuckling of a kenté drum
through the sunlit April of your last afternoon —

(this April, masquerade prancers, moko jumbies,
goatskin drummers aren't allowed to dance
your last parade)

3.
endings. not conclusions. yesterday's memoir. tomorrow's fantasy.
today's fraying edges of old lace.
democracy's partisan tyrannies. logic and reason: assassins hunted.
your tattooed body like a Basquiat graffito. going to fat. distanced and masked.
among supermarket shelves, news of another gone to Sheol.
alone with modest groceries. grown shy of eyes and chatty mouths.
so many fallen apart like brown leaves under breadfruit trees
in the abandoned garden. past passions tune themselves on the car radio
with Marvin Gaye. how see each other again beyond duty and polite
inattention. how fill our lips and arms and legs with each other,
again. endings. memoirs. fantasies. waiting now
for the epiphany of our selves, beyond loneliness, beyond
desire for the passing, the trifling, already forgotten —
endings. not conclusions...

Without Irony

JONATHAN E. HIRSCHFELD

About a year ago Adam Zagajewski wrote to me, and now his words echo as only last words can.

Dear Jonathan,
Today I'm crying for Wojtek Pszoniak who just died. As you know, when you lose a friend there's an avalanche of things that come to your mind.
I knew Wojtek for 70 years, he was like a brother for me.
I've read your essay on Milosz, I like it very much, you've found a way
to capture his essence not only in clay but also in words.
It's a pity that we've lost contact years ago.
Let's hope that--at least--we can be in touch through words. I remember many beautiful moments in your study, with leaf-less trees
outside
or spring trees.
Love to all of your family,
Adam

Last March I received the news that Adam was very ill. Initially there were some grounds for hope, but within barely a few weeks it was over. Suddenly it was I, struggling to restore coherence to my own recollections as he gazed from a pedestal a few meters away. "Leafless trees outside / or spring trees" - this familiar hesitation and this nod to time - Adam's voice.

I have become familiar with this feeling of irrevocable void, but nothing can compress the time it takes to absorb it. My first reflex was to go to the sculpture. When I looked into his eyes, they looked beyond me – or within himself - I couldn't tell. I touched his cheeks, and imagined the air on his skin. I noticed his unusual ears. His tilted, slightly pursed mouth still amused me, and his large baldpate somehow did not age him. From today's perspective he looked young. I could feel irony in the slant of his mouth and the corners where the lips fold inward, and even a hint of humour, but not enough to undermine his sincerity and serenity. I had made him slightly larger than life, perhaps to compensate for his shyness; unconsciously, I think, so he could hold his own next to my Milosz. I imagined the conversation we might have had, decades after having made this. *"We always seek what is gone for good."* (*Another Beauty*)

We met toward the end of the eighties, less than ten years after he had arrived in Paris, and a few years after I had arrived from California. The collapse of the Soviet empire coincided with this period and several of our mutual friends came from Eastern Europe. To a degree that is difficult to imagine today, the times were optimistic. I was touched and amused when he described himself not as a political, but as an erotic, exile who had fled to Paris in pursuit of the woman he loved.

He lived with Maja in a comfortable flat on the western outskirts of the city. It was simple and tasteful, enough for the two of them as well as Maja's daughter, but no more than that. Six for dinner was about the limit. There was a wall of books, and music, and photos, which spoke for themselves. Adam with Brodsky, Walcott, Strand, and of course Milosz. The contrast with Milosz struck me at the time, not only the difference in age, but also a difference in substance. Ann Kjellberg captured it vividly. "He had this eyebrow-cocked devilishness and puckish curiosity that danced a bit above their sometimes ponderous self-understandings. Shyness was perhaps a feature." *(On Adam Zagajewski – Bookpost, 22 3 2021).* Adam was emerging from the shadow of his elder, but, more critically, he was confronted with a different challenge. At a time of intense political change he resisted his Polish contemporaries who believed a writer with his gifts ought to put them in the service of his country, as he had already done very successfully while still in his twenties.

I am reminded of what I saw and felt when I made the sculpture. He looked shy, yet warm, quiet, solitary and contained, watchful, extremely sensitive; a certain stillness. Yet there was also a current of inner motion, as if I could feel his mind at work, or more precisely, his way of sensing the world. This became a conscious theme for the portrait – a state of receptivity and preparedness, even his skin needed to feel like an organ of the senses. Within his way of being I sensed a quiet, determined strength. It took me some time to grasp that this demeanor was a reflection of his conscious urge "to dissent from dissidents". He held true to his contemplative gaze and to an unabashed search for beauty; he could write of the ecstatic and he believed in the soul – this was the form of his resistance, more radical than it might appear. A dissident in the regime of post-modern decline, he wondered how the clay could take that on. And I thought to myself, *only* clay could take that on.

Adam's relationship to those around him was complex. In a poem entitled Self-portrait he told us:
[...]

Sometimes in museums the paintings speak to me and irony suddenly vanishes.
I love gazing at my wife's face.
Every Sunday I call my father.
Every other week I meet with friends,
thus proving my fidelity...
(from 'Mysticism for Beginners' 1997)

This felt like a confession and it surprised me, because Adam showed his fidelity in countless ways. Early on we had shared our appreciation for a proverb that we only knew in English, by Malebranche, a French eighteenth-century religious philosopher: "Attentiveness is the natural prayer of the soul." One day, out of the blue, a fax arrived from Houston with an affectionate note addressed to each of the three of us in my young family, along with a copy of the text in the French original. As I prepared to write this essay I discovered the fax folded into my copy of *Mysticism for Beginners*. Adam was aware that for us these were not idle words. Once Mariana bumped into him at a railway station, as she was accompanying our son to a school for children with special needs. Adam called out to Anton, whom he hardly knew, and embraced him with open arms, as if nothing could ever stand between them.

Adam Zagajewski, polychromed plaster (© Hirschfeld, 1990)

One day Adam asked if we could use my studio as the setting for a documentary about him to be filmed for German television. We had spent many hours together in this luminous space, working against the background chatter of chirping birds that he loved and recognized. There is a sequence in which he meanders through the atelier and settles on the small head of a young boy, for which he felt a particular affection. As I watch this video today I am reminded of his affirmation, with which he concluded his Neustadt lecture in 2004, that *"innocence is perhaps the most daring thing in the entire world."* The camera panned across the collection of portrait heads. Adam was among them. On the shelf they were all equals, memorable for the kind of human beings they were.

Adam's thoughts could take you from Las Meninas in the Prado to Balthus, from Bach to Mahler, sharing his enthusiasms. Yet he was not a snob: *"French intellectuals love to look down their noses at Americans and their boorishness, their lack of taste. France .... frequently fails to understand American enthusiasm. An example: once I was standing before one of the Vermeers in Washington's National Gallery. An American, about forty years old, stood beside me. At one point he turned to me and said (his voice trembled with joy), 'I've been looking at reproductions of this painting since I was twenty, and today I am seeing with my own eyes for the first time. I'm sorry to bother you, but I had to tell someone.' I can take such lack of culture any day."* (Another Beauty)

Once Adam began a university talk with a quotation affirming "It is certainly not the mission of the mind to defend the world dominance of money. Hardly any system was so detrimental to the basic human values as that of capitalism." After describing the police state in which he grew up, he showed his hand. "I hope I have sketched the epistemological situation of someone living in a Communist country clearly enough. And even if this someone – that is, me – would be inclined to adopt a rather aristocratic perspective and to pay homage to artistic and religious imagination rather than to the rules of the free market, he would find it difficult to forget and to renounce his totalitarian experience. Therefore I have no intention of repudiating my old affinity to the human reality as it was described by Balzac. I think I can reveal now that I do not agree with the thesis expressed by Erich Kahler. Yes, it is the mission of the human mind to defend money and the market economy, though it should not be its exclusive and uncritical mission." Adam was his own man.

Expatriates from Eastern Europe were clearly different from their counterparts from North America. Similar things may have enchanted us - the miracle of post-war Western Europe was something to behold - but behind each of us were continents of unshared experience. « *The West Berlin of the early eighties struck me as a peculiar synthesis of the Old Prussian capital and a frivolous city fascinated by Manhattan and the avant-garde (sometimes I suspected that the local intellectuals and artists treated the wall as yet another invention of Marcel Duchamp)"*. (A Defence of Ardour)

When Adam laughed it was as if he was bubbling up from within, literally tickled by his own thoughts. *"I don't see any fundamental contradiction between humour and mystical experience; both serve to wrench us out of our immediate, given reality." (A Defence of Ardour)* I recall a dinner when my wife was bursting with our unborn son. A home video shows Adam playfully tasting the stuffed cabbage and entertaining us with a humorous account of the American feminists that he had only recently discovered in Houston, Texas. As I remember his laughter, I struggle to come to terms with the photos of a much older gentleman that illustrate the eulogies in his memory. Time itself had sculpted my friend. He had matured, and handsomely, but I was grateful to have caught him at a stage when he was still becoming.

Sometimes I felt that Adam and I were like animals from different species that happened to meet by the same river, propelled by a similar thirst. Neither of us had come to Paris by accident but we were bound there, more deeply by love for a person than by love for the place. This made for a mostly unspoken understanding. During one long walk through the city I recall discussing a theme that affected each of us in different ways, the impossibility of witnessing an artist at work. In a conversation with Edward Hirsch he comments on his friendship with Zbigniew Herbert; *"...but we never actually see the person in poetic action, there is this hidden life of the poet, there is something so shameful, or at least very discrete in the poet who is in the act of writing, or inspiration... you never see it. So these friendships are not touching upon the deeper layer..."* (https://podcast.lannan.

org/2009/07/09/adam-zagajewski-with-edward-hirsch/)
In a poem entitled "Poets Photographed", Adam observed that photographs never show the poets *"when they truly see"*, *"never in darkness, never in silence"*, *"at night, in uncertainty, when they hesitate, when joy, like phosphorus, clings to matches."*

The human face is our first landscape. It offers wholeness and unity, even as the idea of the singular human personality has been slowly disintegrating for more than a century. Inner awareness and inner gaze matter as much as the way a person attends to the outside world. The common denominator is consciousness. Often I am trying to reveal something in my portraits that I cannot so much see, as feel. We tend to put the emphasis on vision, as if the key to the art of portraiture is the accuracy of the record. Technique is imitable, but not the synthesis. True essence lies in empathy, the only channel that can reveal the invisible.

For many in Eastern Europe, the question of God is more important than most people living in the West would imagine. One late autumn Adam and Maja presented us with a Christmas gift. Much to our surprise it was a *szopka* that they had brought back from Cracow, a colourful tinfoil model of the nativity scene set inside the entry of the Wawel Cathedral. This is a Polish folk art tradition in which people from all over the country compete for the best model. As they explained this tradition, they shared the place of Catholicism in their lives. At the time I did not feel the weight of this, and we were all aware that there was nothing comparable in our secular Parisian lives. Moreover, Adam was a self-described, failed Catholic, and often underscored his differences with organized religion. But to grasp the aspiration of his art, one must know that he was inhabited by a faith that modern reason has abandoned. In an interview some years later, I read Adam's attempt to explain the resistance to his work that he encountered in France. He described a conversation with a French poet on a visit to Poland, who told him quite simply, "There is only one thing that astonishes me when I read Polish poetry. When I read your poems -not just yours - I see that you still have a problem with God. In France we decided it's a childish question. It doesn't exist." With typical wit Adam added, "I won't tell you his name. Maybe he wouldn't be saved." *(Interview with Alice Quinn, 2009 The New Salon).*

To make a portrait sculpture of a friend is an innocent pursuit, but not without risks. Rarely do we see others the way their loved ones see them. The time spent together, one contemplating the other, leads to a strange objectivity. It is very difficult to see clearly those to whom we are attached. We sometimes want things to be different from the way they are. And yet there is nothing like caring deeply to open up the senses and to feel we know things without knowing why.

Roarer and other poems

KATHRYN PALLANT

The tea chests

arrive unannounced,
empty.

Splinter wood
with metal seams metal tacked,

lined with crinkled tin and the dead
rose scent of darjeeling.

At night I lie
rigid with reluctance to move.

Into them we lower our small
sacred things:

Water Babies,
LPs, a doll's horse but not her house.

The chests press against the
speechless piano,

the table's dropped
leaves. An unlinked chain of chairs

cleaves space with the blunder violence
of cows corralled at market.

Our mother collects us
in the middle of a mid-term day. I leave

a comic strip behind for my father. He
values funny things.

Roarer

Being of the demographic,
I heard a man on Woman's Hour
bemoan the menopause,
the unfortunate effects
of his wife's unbearable rage.

Her whereabouts
went unmentioned
but he was there for her
in a soundproof studio.

I too have seen her—
iron woman unhinged
striding aroar across
the burnt out gorse
of the moors,

decrying the terraces
snaking the valley,
meek gardens,
man caves.

Hinze Dam

*'The first time I saw Ted Hughes was on a school trip to
Hebden Bridge, where he read his poems in a moth-eaten
cinema.'* – Simon Armitage

Ted fucking Hughes
in the theatre at Hebden Bridge,
reading to the flick haired boys
in the flip back plush seat
of history, the free gift
of his country, where among cold
kitchens and smuts there's gold.

Where was my Ted Hughes,
my Elmet (not Elnett)
at Palm Beach High?
Where's the coal seam soul
of my place, my epiphany
in the screwed up sweet papers,
the flight to language sung
from mind to tongue, let loose over
slagscapes and dormant chimneys?

You know who we had?
Russ Hinze, whose name
was on the local dam. It burst
its banks one year in just the way
his bulbous buttocks flooded
the bucket chairs at assembly:
the progressive bloat of authority.

I left that year with my air-filled head,
sun blistered nose and robust health,
aimless in the sticky air, sixteen
and sick of it. For Hughes
Haworth's just over Dales,
but in Queensland it's fantasy fiction.
Even in a book shop – try to find one
between bars and bikinis –
it's out of my modest reach:

abroad the struggle's with Thatcher,
but not even she slapped tax on books.
The thought fox is coming but not here,
better to seek the sublime at the surf club,
raise a XXXX to Hughes (never bitter),
even read him, but never hear him murmur
his verse for us into the velvet dark.

See Also and other poems

AMY ACRE

The Year of the Horse

after Giles Goodland

Twentysomethings geeked out over the World Wide Web
while polyamorous malware circled in hoodies.

Green-collar workers looked for a connection between hand gel
and transmissible spongiform encephalopathies.

Thatcher toppled like a graven image and I wrote a school news
report on her fall, gleefully dictated by my mum.

I met a large grey bear in a South London hospital. Microplastic
props accumulated in McMansions. Dad died.

The crime wave was high with muggings mysterious. Earth
waited for a shout-out from air formerly known as wall.

I would have given anything for a stick blender, or a soundbar,
or a black hat, or a lithium-ion battery.

Fine Music

the rabbi's daughter let me try on her swimsuit
while our parents drank in the garden

led me to the bathroom, said the suit was waterproof
you could wee straight through so i did and she watched

before we ran to the depths of the blow-up pool
and when i think of this i think of her father leading me

through a door, him asking how it would feel
on the bimah, no father to applaud

of saying 'empty' – my careful picking
the performance more exact than my big day

noting the smudge, when as sometimes happens we are called upon
to give away our stream to make fine music of our pain

See Also

Dad is a see also of mum. Mum is a see also of dad.
As nouns the difference between mum and dad is that
mum is (chiefly|uk|informal) mother or **mum** can be a
chrysanthemum or mum can be (obsolete) silence or **mum**
can be a sort of strong beer, originally made in brunswick,
germany while **dad** is (informal) a father, a male parent.

As an adjective mum is (colloquial) silent.
As an interjection mum is stop speaking! hush!.
As a verb mum is to act in a pantomime or dumb show.

Ali Talks Me Through the Multiverse

I've been trying to tell this story for a long time.
I remember holding my infant father in my arms.
I couldn't save him. But once you've heard the clang
-snap of an assault rifle being gathered you'll know it
on every street you walk. Our bodies are at war
with us forever and all I got was this lousy t-shirt.

I am always walking into rooms as if I'm walking out of them.

Rachel's brain used to take her away, sometimes just
a few seconds, mid-castling, a falling tonic of chess
pieces and I always wondered where she went,
if it was like Laura Palmer in the Black Lodge.

There is a universe where you ate Coco Pops
instead of Shreddies. There is a universe where
you wore boots and, lacing, missed your train.
There is a universe where you caught the train
and it was hit by a crashing Dornier. There is

a universe where you exploded, blood hitting the air like stars.

At primary, Mr Eccles was everyone's favourite
teacher, warm and kind and, of course, he died young.
The school gave a weekly award in his name. Years
later, stories came out. Strange touching during PE.
Wrong unworded things, a live fish in your hand,
dead fox on the school run. What do we do with that?

Over Pinot on Zoom, Ali talks me through the multiverse.

Before we were mothers, we were people. Drunk
on the carpet in devil horns, lying to the chorus.

When I look for David, he is standing behind the glass
of a new-build office that looks out on a city sidestreet.
It's Bring Your Kids to Work Day and we're typing notes
to each other on Acorn Computers, alien green
on federal black. I try to pick him out through the floor-
to-ceiling windows but the glass is flushed with sunlight,

I only see myself. I don't know which one of us is inside.

The Thames by Night

HORATIO MORPURGO

'Wherever the storm carries me, I land as a guest'
Horace

The painter, a Belgian refugee, welcomed his friend and added some final touches before handing over the canvas. The friend's wife had given birth earlier that day – this could only be a flying visit – but walking to the window, he held this gift up to the light, admiring, and promised to take care of it. This was April 1918. The building in which that artist rented his space is long-gone. The newly-arrived child was my grandmother by the time I met her, sitting in an armchair at the far end of the century. She had been an actress once. There were publicity shots and stories about her beautiful reading voice. But I knew her as a watchful, elderly enigma and the picture as a kind of companion piece to that enigma.

She had her strange name, Kippe, from a Belgian village which was the scene of an important battle fought the same day. *The Thames by Night* had hung in every home she'd ever lived in. It hung at last above the fireplace in a converted mews in Shepherd's Bush, where I finally came to know her as well as I ever would.

His arm in hers, grandfather Jack shuffled at her side as she steered him across the front room after supper. On arrival at his armchair, she murmured something and he let go, felt for the arm-rests, then turned and dropped gamely between them, reaching for his cigarettes as he did so. Kippe fetched him a glass of vodka and then sat down herself, smoking from her own packet and sipping a soft drink. A thick nicotine haze spread through the room. Steeped so long in these fumes, that moonlight on the Thames had by now acquired a yellow-ish look.

The news about our grandparents was generally news about Jack's eyesight: operations, diabetes, what 'tunnel vision' means. He had been in his time a soldier and a PR man, an editor and a professor, writer of travel books and the Pelican *History of the United States*, a radio personality. But I was full of irreverence – as were we all – for our duty of... was it his stories we inhaled and his smoke we listened to or the other way?

We'd been raised, in any case, less on the public intellectual and his accolades than on the accumulated hurt here, on the difficulties of the marriage (Kippe's second). We knew about the damage done at all those corners he had cut as a spouse, parent and step-parent. We were raised on that soft drink she always sipped, after bringing him the vodka. Sometimes, as he talked, she would take a pull on her cigarette and you saw her eyes narrow a fraction, as if smarting, as if you'd caught her in the act of weighing some word of his very carefully. On its way to the husband of five decades, now so very dependent, her pointed glance flitted past the yellowing moonlight.

So much for what we knew, or thought we did. But this was also a house full of things you didn't yet know and as such held out the promise of some future date at which you might know them. Years after he was able to read any of them, Jack continued to receive new titles from the publishing companies he'd worked for. It must have been Kippe who shelved them. The place was books from floor to ceiling, spare room included. A literary cavern piled high with treasures of the mind: to my earliest self, this was a storehouse of wisdom. I don't remember now how I reconciled such contradictory views of the place but I do recall the moment I first became aware of that contradiction as a problem I needed to resolve.

They somehow contrived also to be the kind of grandparents who take you on foreign holidays. And as it was in their own front room, so it was abroad, or indeed when they came to see me at university: Kippe murmuring 'up' or 'down' at each curb as we walked the town, his hand always on her arm. In the foyer of the hotel where they stayed in Cambridge, Jack wordlessly handed her his glasses. As she polished them with a little yellow cloth, something struck me about that familiar gesture, seen afresh in this new context. How little attention I'd ever paid to the way they were together, to all that passed, every day, like this, unspoken between them. I was twenty, in other words, before it occurred to me that I'd only ever seen these two through the stories I'd been told about them by other people.

I wrote a poem about her cleaning his glasses and then handing them back. It won a prize, so I proudly copied it out for them as their next Christmas present. They hung it on the wall in their front room, next to a poem by Kippe's father. During the years after university, when I used their house as a London stop-over on my travels, there that poem always was. They had spent enough time around students, I guess, to understand how encouragement works.

Until then I'd responded to *The Thames by Night*, also, more through the stories about it, how it came to be 'ours', than through the picture itself. Exposure to thick cigarette smoke had certainly dimmed it over the years, but I began to realise now what a fine painting it was in its own right.

The view was said to be from the Embankment, though nobody seemed to know exactly where. On a Thames ablaze with reflected lunar glare, irregular shapes floated – barges moored in midstream, reduced here to black bars, each one blocking that reflection in its own way. Closer inshore, smoke was rising from the funnel of a steam tug. Its smoke, drifting upwards, became entangled in the branches of a young river-side tree. Here and there, you couldn't quite distinguish the moon-lit smoke from the blurred grey beginnings of foliage along the tree's branches.

Only now did I also notice the people in it. Could these, I wondered, be the finishing touches which had been put to the picture before it was handed over? A loosely daubed couple stood beneath that tree, the limbs of which were so curiously involved with coal smoke. These two, then, as well myself looking at the picture, we were all observers of the scene. What else had I missed here all these years, if I had missed them?

*

Both were from backgrounds marked by recent migration – her father was the Belgium poet Emile Cammaerts, both of his parents were Dutch. Her father's English was never completely fluent but he was a translated poet and his work had appeared with the Bodley Head. He was also a published historian with a university job. His status was relatively secure. Her mother, Tita Brand, had been a successful actress and remained an overbearing figure. Kippe's aspiration to follow her onto the stage had to contend with her mother's formidable intellectual snobbery – and perhaps insecurity. Kippe might be the family beauty but it didn't always work in her favour. Her earlier divorce was not easily forgiven: this was long before the 'cultural sector' was ever invented, never mind the 'creative industries'. We forget how morally precarious the theatre once was. A brother she'd been close to, an actor also and ally in her struggles, was killed during the war, a loss which confirmed the family's turn to religion.

Jack had taken a more active part in distancing himself from family. His parents, married in an Amsterdam synagogue, converted to Anglicanism on arrival in London, where their children were born. Jack was baptised and later sang in the choir of an East End church. He could overplay at times the extent of this true-born Englishness: not unheard of from second-generation immigrants and perhaps not that surprising from a war veteran. He was ashamed of lower-middle class origins and in playing them down also played down a Jewish background.

But I mentioned foreign holidays: they once spent several months in Israel while he completed his autobiography. He went, in that book, to far more trouble than was necessary to avoid all mention of his parents' origins. But why, then, finish writing it there of all places? And why invite me along? I for my part chose to see that view of the walls of Jerusalem, that trip to Jericho, as his way of saying as much as he wanted to. I still think saying more might have done him good. He, manifestly, disagreed. Or he never talked about it and I – why? – never asked.

A best guess: he grew up in the East End at a time when the question of how Jewish communities should relate to European nation-states was, everywhere, more and more urgent. I have on my shelf school prizes he was awarded in 1936, the year of the Battle of Cable Street. Across the continent, minorities were viewed more and more as a security risk. As his parents' answer, perhaps, had been to get their children baptized, so his own, in a way, was to edit Charles Lamb. But that feels a bit reductive. We never discussed it so I'm speculating still.

In any case, by the time I got to know them well, it felt right that the centrepiece of their front room should be so emphatically hers, hers from birth. Some of the books had belonged to her father but most of them were Jack's, and most of the stories, too, were his. So that picture adjusted the room's atmosphere, brought it closer to the current situation. When Kippe talked it might be about her acting days or about her lost brother or about her father's poetry. More often, as if relieved to have Jack's restless mind occupied, she watched and she listened and then she went to bed.

It felt like being on fire duty. The load of ash would steadily build at the tip of his cigarette as he became absorbed in a story. Lost in reminiscence, he waved his hand about while I agonised over when to interrupt. I never found a way to get this right. Kippe would have murmured one of her something-almost-nothings, and he'd have realised at once, but when I did it, it always felt like interrupting. When you did eventually say, he'd pause before irritably tapping the ash anywhere except in the tray provided. Some of it might land on the carpet so then you watched that. He rested his hand on my arm later as I guided him to the foot of the stairs, then gripped the banister and was all right going up on his own.

The Thames by Night was right for that room for another reason. They were both of them Londoners without apology, the first I ever knew. Jack claimed never to have understood exactly 'what anybody *does* in the countryside', putting on a sly face as he asked for clarification. It made Kippe laugh, too. Having grown up there of course, in the countryside, I did 'understand'. I expected to end up living there, too, but had questions about that by now, so their 'perplexity' was an invitation to speak freely and I was grateful. Their native city was, for them, all about strangers and access to elsewhere and the truth was that I, too, by now wanted as much of both as I could get as they perhaps understood.

Jack had read Charles Lamb early and the London he adored was largely created in the essayist's image. I guess even the addiction to tobacco owed something to that 'little smoky room at the Salutation and Cat' which he was always talking about. It was the room in a pub where Lamb and friends lit their pipes and ate 'welch Rabbits' while they talked poetry and the 'golden days to come on earth' and that perfectly egalitarian community they would found in the American Midwest just as soon as they got there. 'Elia' was, in effect, how this son of Dutch immigrants naturalised. It was through his identification with Lamb that he began to make his own mark as a writer and editor after the war.

He referred me to a letter his hero once wrote to William Wordsworth, in which the cockney defends his home town and city life with it. His attachments to 'old chairs, old tables, streets, squares where I have sunned myself' meant no less to him than a countryman's surroundings. The same 'well-natured alchemy' can find instruction in 'the common incidents of town-life' just as it can in the countryside, for 'the mind can make friends with anything.'

Can it? Well, that's what conversation is for, and we had those conversations. Jack's communicative nature, and the love of literary London which was a part of that, found employment through the career he loved to talk about. What could sound like narcissism – and had, as such, grated on his children – wasn't only that. Once you stopped dreading those stories, you soon started hearing it: his love of the world city that had made him.

I stopped over on my way to America or Greece, India or Australia, and always there was a meal and there were memories, recommendations, travel tips. It's not, in other words, the family enmities or the smell of tobacco I remember now about that place, though I know it reeked of both. Or rather it is those but also the book-lined den I recall, late-night conversations in a house which was, in effect, my ante-room to the planet. It is the suitcase packed upstairs and the flight tomorrow and two well-disposed elders both sharing in my anticipation.

*

But it was she who had the heart by-pass and in the end it was she, on one of their many trips, who didn't wake up one morning in an American hotel. The easiest place for the family to gather awkwardly to mark this was the atrium of a Marriot outside Heathrow. It was the first time I'd lost a close relative. All I remember is staring at a fully grown transplanted palm tree.

I was by then occupying rented rooms in one city after another, reading a lot, picking up my first work as a journalist. Jack was still there when I moved to London a few years later and still in the same house. A live-in Ukrainian help cooked meals and talked to him. There my poem still was, by the empty armchair one hesitated to occupy. There was *The Thames by Night*. I was as welcome as ever, if not more so. And I went to see him less often than I should have.

His shortcomings as a family man forty years earlier were my rock and my salvation. Now that it suited me to, I wondered whether his children and stepchildren might not have been right about him, after all. How readily I enlisted family grievances that were not my own, how I chose to remember the egotism I had never myself experienced. Now that it suited me to. Lear said it best: 'Age is unnecessary.'

He was more forgetful than ever about those cigarettes. Back on fire duty, I remember wincing as the ash cascaded down the side of grey flannel trousers. It did no harm but was it *sensitivity* on my part to say nothing? Or regulation twenty-something reluctance to take responsibility for anything? Responsibility was what live-in Ukrainians were for. So, he might be in Greece again or drinking vodka with the Russians in Teheran or half-way up Italy in 1943 and I'd watch him lighting the cigarette half-way along or less, no longer able to judge where the end of it was. I even suspected him of doing it on purpose. That is what a rotten conscience does for you.

What stories I had to tell him 'back', my trips to report on this or that, aroused little interest. As I complained grandly of my ill-treatment by some editor, it felt unkind of him to quote Lamb at me: "T'is cold work, Authorship, without something to puff one into fashion.' But looking back, as I often now do, I can see he was only trying to move the conversation on, yes, in the direction of something he knew about, but he thought I should know about it, too.

Lamb, for him – I get it now – was the patron saint of London freelancers. The Penguin selection he edited in the late Forties, and dedicated to Kippe, was his way to help with the rebuilding of his city. In the 1990s he adapted it for Carcanet. It was his last book and he dedicated it to Kippe again. With his eyesight as it was by then, she must have done most of the work.

Their generation, of course, was no longer at the helm. He couldn't help with contacts or anything like that. But Lamb had known all about authors and their struggles and Jack could pass that on, or try to. He would tell me again about those 'golden days to come on earth' which the essayist and friends had believed in. About the open evenings he and his sister held on Wednesdays, at their lodgings in Mitre Court. How Hazlitt, Wordsworth and Coleridge had made up the charmed circle. Leigh Hunt, the editor who discovered Shelley and Keats, was a regular. Jack's very first publication had been a new edition of Leigh Hunt's autobiography.

He gave me a first edition of George Dyer, that life-long 'framer of immortal commonwealths', a neighbour, another close friend of Lamb's, who also supplied Coleridge with his London introductions when nobody knew who he was.

It was years before I worked out what Jack had meant by all this. A blind old man, alone and housebound, recalling a London in which people met and drank and teased and talked and entertained wild hopes. My wilful blindness and the way I justified it at the time set me a problem I only began to solve years later, a long way from London by then.

What I can see now is that he shaped for himself, from knowing his way so well around the exchanges and relationships between those writers, a replacement for the city he had lost. Their conversations formed a sort of parallel or fourth dimension into which he could slip at any time. Lamb spoke of the imagination as his 'barricade against despair' and I think this more or less locked-in emeritus professor came to know, better than any of us ever wants to, what that meant.

Not that I completely missed the point at the time. If 'the mind can make friends with anything' and he, a blind old man, still knew that, then couldn't I, young and healthy, cheer up a bit? Were my prospects really so bleak? He gave me a subscription to *PN Review*, which eventually took three poems I sent them. Lamb had published some of his best work in the *London Magazine*, which was still running, so far as Jack knew. The *London Magazine* sent back quite a few things before they accepted one. I went to read it to Jack as soon as I heard because I knew he'd be pleased.

And he was, I think. As he would have been, of course, if I'd dropped round more often even without something to boast about. I suppose his loneliness frightened me, reminded me too sharply of my own. I felt ashamed of my slow start. Or I easily found ways to justify the neglect, rather. At such a crucial juncture of my life, how baffling that he should be alone and then get ill. I was off on a trip at the time but luckily Jack was a permanent fixture. He wasn't going anywhere.

He went anyway, so I was abroad when I heard, pointlessly tinkering with the latest broken-down relationship. You could be not readily contactable in those days for weeks if you chose. I was depressed and I did choose. I therefore missed his funeral and had more than one reason to be feeling wretched by the time I got back to London.

The front room was being picked over by book dealers but not many of the books I wanted were gone. We could take what we liked, and I filled three boxes. Under the stairs were the items left specifically in the will, among them, for me, the poem by Kippe's father. To the frame of *The Thames by Night* was also attached a post-it note with my name on it.

The writing and teaching and even the broadcasting never made much money. The house had been paid for out of my uncle's earnings in insurance. Jack's anecdotes of encounters with the famous were, by the end, mainly an occasion for the exchanging of rueful glances. But he'd said he wrote for George Orwell's *Tribune* and I went to look it up once. He did write for Orwell's *Tribune*. He'd heard T.S. Eliot reading his own poetry, in a voice, he said, 'like a bank manager turning down an application for a mortgage.' He always said he had corresponded with Siegfried Sassoon, another writer unsure what to do with his Jewish background. Now here, taped inside the back cover of his copy of the *Selected Poems*, was Sassoon's letter to a 'Mr Morpurgo', about war poetry.

For him literature was above all *collaborative* and *urban*. It was about editors, deadlines, galley proofs, the risk of prosecution. It was about print as contestation. He was proud to have been made a professor without

studying for a PhD. The war and then a job in publishing were all the 'post-grad' studies he had needed. A short story sent from the North African desert, published in *Penguin New Writing*, was all his introduction to post-war literary London. I guess he never forgot how precarious beginnings can feel and that's why he lent me the support which I did not repay very generously. His tattered copy of that magazine matters as much, now, as anything else I carried out of that house.

You never of course feel these things as and when you should. That these insights arrive long after they are much use to anyone feels, obscurely, like part of their function and fascination. At the time it was with other feelings entirely that I packed my inheritance into the back of a car I was sleeping in at the time. What if my attachment to all this was the problem? Theirs had, after all, been an unhappy marriage. Jack's restlessness and his egotism had damaged other people, not just himself. Wasn't there a non-literary lesson here, a conclusion it was high time I drew?

The phase of my life that had opened in that front room was ending in disarray. This house had been part library, part launch-pad, part affirmation filling-station. How could I not grieve for the loss of those who had made all that available to me? But what if my attachment to this book-lined literary grotto was part of the problem now? What if it had tripped me up, left me forever out of step with now? I left the painting till last so that it would go on top of everything else. As I picked it up, I turned it round to see if anything was written on the back.

The Thames by Night: that title had been firmly lodged in my mind for as long as I could remember. But I must have made it up. The painting was called *Reverberations of a March Morning*. It was the sun, through smog and nicotine tar, and not the moon, which illuminated this scene. It was a picture about the morning, not the night. I'd missed the most elementary truth about it. And they'd left it to me anyway.

Reviews

A Mappemonde

Miles Burrows, *Take Us the Little Foxes*: *collected poems* (Carcanet) £14.99
Reviewed by N.S. Thompson

In a 1962 essay 'The Creative Process', James Baldwin wrote, 'A society must assume that it is stable, but the artist must know, and he must let us know, that there is nothing stable under heaven.' Indeed, as he says in the same essay, 'the artist must be an incorrigible disturber of the peace'. One way he or she may do this, as Wallace Stevens wrote in *The Necessary Angel*, is by 'the imagination pressing back against the pressure of reality'. The most obvious way the imagination can do this is by presenting some kind of heightened or altered state over everyday reality, but that would be to regress into Romanticism or the many *-isms* that followed it. Miles Burrows has long created his own mischievous form of disruption and now gathers the results in his collected poems, *Take Us The Little Foxes*, just over half a century after he was discovered at a reading in London by Cape editor Tom Maschler, who subsequently published a first volume in 1966, *A Vulture's Egg*. Bizarrely, the world had to wait five decades for a second collection, perhaps aptly titled *Waiting for the Nightingale* (2017), published by Carcanet, whose publisher Michael Schmidt is acknowledged for the present volume not as a necessary angel, perhaps, but even more as a 'Deus ex machina'.

However, it is not as if the poet had been living in obscurity, rather a life stretched to the full as a medical practitioner in various parts of the world, both as a GP and a psychiatrist. He had also achieved wide recognition in Edward Lucie Smith's Penguin anthology *British Poetry Since 1945* (1970), which included his memorably

witty 'minipoet' in the 'Post-Movement' section:

> – slim, inexpensive, easy to discard
> nippy rather than resonant, unpretentious.
> we found them produced in increasing numbers
> from oxford, home of pressed steel.

This 'nippy' little poet is contrasted with the traditional 'lumbering', 'well-upholstered' figure of the 'archpoet', whom 'we had to coax, persuade him he had wings'. More than a dig at the Movement poets, as Lucie-Smith assumes, it also prods at the sleek new 60s freedom from form and escape from the confines of capital letters. This early example shows the rhythmic conversational mode that saves his work from the plod into which so much free verse descends. Indeed, here he copies the sprightly mode and direct address of the advertising copywriter.

But it was not always thus. The lower case dig at Oxford belies the truth that he spent many years there, firstly as an undergraduate reading Greats (classics) and then Medicine. In fact, his first book reflects that first degree in the many references to the Latin poets and the matter of Troy in particular. There is a striking variety of forms, ranging from beautifully well-wrought sonnets to quatrains that could well have come out of the Movement, to dialogues, squibs and even a dramatic dialogue in the style of Beckett in 'Detective Story':

Lady:	The unfortunate lodger is dead.
Boy:	Unfortunately, the lodger is dead.
Interpreter:	The lodger is dead, unfortunately.
Inspector:	The dead lodger is unfortunate.

As this example shows, the salient feature of Burrows's work is its obliquity. Appropriating the term from astronomy, in *Obliquity* (2010) the economist David Kay defined it as 'characteristic of systems that are complex, imperfectly understood, and change their nature as we engage with them'. This seems the best description of the kaleidoscopic way this poet aims to disturb the peace and throw a curved ball at it. Another take on Emily Dickinson's 'Tell all the truth but tell it slant'? Not really. Dickinson expected some truth eventually to be revealed. More pertinent perhaps is her following line 'Success in circuit lies.' Burrows's successful vision lies in the tangential, without any hankering after a solid circle on which the tangent rests. And yet the circle often feels solid from the vast range of the poet's references. A good example from *Waiting for the Nightingale* is 'The Flight from Meaning':

> Doreen looked back at me, her face like a Tacitus
>   unseen.
> I like difficult poets who tease you, difficult girls
> Pulling their hair over their faces and running away.
> Though this could get tiresome.
> Soon it will be time to cycle through the rain to yoga.
> I wish I was mysterious.
> All I wanted was to be opaque and cryptic.

The persona's aspiration here is fully borne out in the whole collection, which adds up to an oblique critique of poetry itself, undermining its standard tropes and observations. Looking over the privet hedge of our insular gentility, 'English Provincial Poetry' is a devastatingly tongue-in-cheek list of Dos and Don'ts. One can also note the gradual incursion into the poetry of genteel female figures that seem to have escaped from the talking heads of Alan Bennett: Doreen, Madge, Glynis and Daphne to mention a few.

One of the collection's most opaque and cryptic set of references is in the title poem 'Take Us the Little Foxes'. We learn from a footnote that the *Song of Solomon* 'suddenly interrupts itself with an instruction about catching little foxes' because, as the Song itself says (2:15), they 'spoil the vines: for our vines have tender grapes'. The footnote goes on to say this reference has had many mystical and erotic interpretations, but that others believe it is a 'practical instruction for market gardeners'. This humour reflects the poem's subtly humorous interplay of times and people. It starts with the Natural History Group in the (Sinai?) desert, the Queen of Sheba's palace being 'somewhere round here'. The speaking voice then becomes the Queen herself waiting for Solomon's visit, a Solomon who becomes Bob Dylan and they discuss many things, including her famous *Arrival* (*pace* Handel). We then understand this meeting could have been imagined by a Dr Ruffidge of the Natural History Group, but the voice becomes Sheba again talking to Sol(omon) as if both were living New Yorkers and she even 'sings' the King James's translation of verse 2:15. Finally we end on the Natural History Group returning home, not having found the Palace of the Queen, but with the voice over of a beautiful fade:

> From the minarets in the town far below
> Came the sound of tannoyed imprecations.
> As darkness fell
> The mosques were bathed in flickering green
>   lights, suggesting horror films.
> But for the Bedu, the flickering green
> Suggested grass, green pastures, calmer moods.

These shifts are deft and harmonious and always held together by a speaking voice. We never imagine the poet labouring over an impersonal description, it comes from a voice that is always embedded in a setting. But a setting that turns and changes in a kaleidoscopic manner, calling just about everything into question with wit, erudition and often laugh-out-loud humour as it most incorrigibly disturbs the peace. And for this reviewer the real tour-de-force of the collection is the almost parody of Wallace Stevens's 'Sea Surface Full Of Clouds' in 'Wallace in Undieland':

> Her made to measure mental camisole
> Fluffed a little at the edges, holds
> Suggestions of Byzantium, in green,
> Its acrobatic hemlines, year by year,
> Trace with acutest sighs a mappemonde.
> Phenomenal cadenzas of the real!

Phenomenal they may be, but we are made to question the reality of that 'real' in the most engaging and oblique manner.

Reopened Eyes

Jamie McKendrick, *The Foreign Connection: Writings on Poetry, Art and Translation* (Legenda) £75
Reviewed by Chris Miller

Let's begin with Naiads, surfacing for a prodigious spectacle: Argo, the first ship. Now to Dante, for whom a single point in all that he has learned in Paradiso is more trouble to expound than the twenty-five centuries since Neptune was amazed at the inaugural navigation. Here, it is Catullus's *Nereides admirantes* from his epyllion (64:15); there, his echo is heard in *Paradiso* XXXIII.96, *che fe' Nettuno ammirar l'ombra d'Argo.* Time has passed, not quite that between the Argo and Dante, but enough for Catullus's works to have been cast into one seemingly perpetual night; they re-emerged in Verona in time for Dante's residence there. So there are grounds for thinking that this is not coincidence. That merest point – *un punto solo m'e maggior letargo* – has its own progeny: in Tasso's *La Gerusalemme Liberata*, God looks down on the earth *e in un sol punto, e in una / vista mirò ciò ch'in sé il mondo aduna* ('And in a single point, and one / glance saw that which the world contains in itself', I.vii.7–8). This is a beautiful vein of poetic continuity, if rightly seen.   Is it rightly seen? None of the Dante scholars, 'steeped in the Classics', as McKendrick rightly says, acknowledges Dante's debt to Catullus. The Nereids stand *nutricum tenus exstantes e gurgite cano,* in Michie's translation 'nipple-naked in the grey-green swell', while Neptune sees the Argo float over his head in Dante.

Admirantes / ammirar unite Catullus and Dante. Dante's *un punto solo* becomes *in un sol punto*; Neptune's upward amazement becomes God's downward all-seeing. Dante's 'single point' is a point of argument, yoked to an ocean of time. The *sol punto* of God's vision is a universe, not an article of theology, yet that connection to the vision of Neptune feels, to me, undeniable.

No certainty is available in this case. But when Dante writes: *Sopra candido vel cinta d'oliva / Donna m'apparve, sotto verde manto, / Vestita di color di fiamma viva* ('in an olive-girdled white veil / a woman appeared to me, in a green cloak / dressed in the colour of living flame') and is echoed in Sonnet 190 by Petrarch in *Una candida cerva sopra l'erba / verde m'apparve, ... / fra due riviere, all'ombra d'un alloro* ('A white deer upon the green / grass appeared before me ... / between two rivers, in the shadow of a laurel tree'), surely the case is clearer, though it takes a particular sensibility to spot the sequence 'sopra candido... m'apparve... verde' reversed in Petrarch as 'candida... sopra... verde m'apparve' – and thence point forward to Wyatt.

Lest these examples seem remote, McKendrick is no less felicitous in observing the 'militaristic terminology' of Michael Hofmann's 'Pastorale' from *Corona, Corona*, the 'alphabetic chiasmus' of its last line ('ancillary, bacillary blocks of anthrax') and the 'unhappy collision of gender attributes' in the rhyming line 'six-pack of Feminax', or noting that Blake is a 'prototype of the *flâneur*' in 'I wandered through the chartered streets, / near where the chartered Thames doth flow'. This sensibility is combined with wit. In a longer essay on 'Bishop's Birds', McKendrick focuses on Elizabeth Bishop's 'The Sandpiper', adducing its relation to Blake and to Baudelaire's 'L'Albatros' and showing how the sandpiper ('the peculiar kind of seeing that the bird is capable of is at once a miraculous magnification and a comic occlusion') can become an avatar of the poet, though 'it is typical of Bishop that the bard should take a back seat to the bird'.

Such observation might be the property of either the poet or the translator of poetry, two roles in which McKendrick has excelled. And, indeed, a number of these essays concern translation – not least of Dante, but also of Pavese, Montale, Pasolini, Enzensberger, Anedda, Magrelli, Grünbein, and Bassani, whose *Romanzo di Ferrara* he has translated. Others deal with near-contemporaries, such as Heaney, Mahon, Paulin, Muldoon, Bernard O'Donoghue (the Irish connection is strong) Hofmann, and twentieth-century classics such as Hughes, Lowell and Keith Douglas.

McKendrick is also an artist and many essays here consider the fine-arts, sometimes in their interaction with poetry; the essay cited above about Catullus and Dante begins with the Latin poet's influence on Titian; Botticelli's Dante is also examined, as is Michelangelo's poetry. Other painters were new to me, notably the French miniaturist Jean Bourdichon (1457/9–1521), whose delightfully knowing *Bathsheba* (Getty Collection, online) bathes in the lines of her blazons. McKendrick judiciously reappraises painters such as C. R. W. Nevinson and Paul Nash, some of whose work is close to my heart without always impressing the critical intellect. What is one to make of the semi-abstract landscape-sublime of Wilhelmina Barns-Graham? The St Ives exhibition of 2000 afforded McKendrick the opportunity to rehearse her career; that essay, in characteristic fashion, returns you to his subject re-enthused and eyes re-opened.

This book might have been written for my pleasure. Many readers of this journal will surely feel the same. There will be a paperback.

Confidence

Much with Body, Polly Atkin (Seren) £9.99
Reviewed by Charlotte Wetton

Confidence is my first impression of Polly Atkin's *Much with Body*, which is perhaps to be expected from the author of a second collection and 'several pamphlets'. There's a confidence in placing *Full Wolf Moon* first in the collection – a poem with a limited, repetitive yet highly effective vocabulary. And there's confidence in stepping directly from this to 'Hunting the Stag', with its uneven line and verse lengths. This poem initially appears to have been thrown on the page by an amateur but unfolds with great tonal surety. Her phrasing rings true on the ear whilst simultaneously opening up phrases to a wider interpretation, such as 'You know what you become when you're like this. Too much. Too much.'

Confidence in form is seen in *Dorothy's Rain,* a three-page poem in which practically every other word is rain, and the spacing echoes the pattern of rain drops. With such devices immediately obvious to the eye, I steeled myself not to skip, but to read every word and to go along with Atkin on this experiment. And the poem did deliver, even more on the ear than the eye, a mesmeric torrent, an interrogation of language and a beautiful evocation of the human experience of place. Even the unpromising blocky stanzas of *The Long Dance* seem to open and flex as the poem progresses, whilst still holding their shape. Likewise, the incantatory poem *Queen of the Woods* uses line spacing to continually soften and extend the line into a hypnotic flow. Atkin is a master of enjambment, making the most wrenching of line-breaks feel natural, even when she is playing with double meanings. Every turn of the page refreshes the reader with a change of form that never feels forced or showy. There are found poems aplenty, a cento and an aubade but each feels exactly right for itself, without rigidity. This winning combination of tone and form makes for sure-footed, deliberate poems. The reader is drawn into each poem-world, particularly in section 1, the most imaginatively engaging section, with its images of frogs in the house and bears in the library, somehow both otherworldly and instantly recognisable.

Atkin needs to be confident because she is treading well-worn ground: Dorothy Wordsworth, Grasmere, a troubled identification with a changing natural world. The third section deals with long term pain and illness, and this, too, has been written about, increasingly, in recent years. Theme-wise this *is* very much a 2021 book. But Atkins does find something new to say about these places and experiences. The collection might have been stronger without the guard-rails which separate the poems into the three sections, and which group the poems solely by content. There might have been a more interesting way of structuring the book which brought out connections between human and environmental pain, between care and the visceral embodiment which are features of both sections 1 and 3. As it is, the shorter section 2 is somewhat marooned as the poor relation in the middle. Section 2 also has some very similar poems which aren't served well by being side by side. The same desire to make things navigable for the reader is seen in the poem *Notes from a Transect*; the subtitles here do nothing but get in the way. But really, I'm quibbling. Even if you're not interested in pain or in the Grasmere weather system, you'll still enjoy *Much with Body*.

'I'm already there'

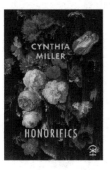

Honorifics, Cynthia Miller (Nine Arches Press) £9.99
Reviewed by Annie Fan

Cynthia Miller's debut, *Honorifics*, has won an Eric Gregory award and been shortlisted for the Forward Prize for Best First Collection. The book moves us between time and place, from Malaysia to America to the UK, searching for a form or language to hold a specific kind of longing: for another self, another country, what might have been. It would be unfair to ask women and people of colour to provide universal delight; as a woman of colour, Miller's longing is one specific to the experience of migration and of heritage with gendered burdens. The title of the collection is a paean to this, deriving from the poem 'Glitch Honorifics' where 'coming back to / Malaysia feels like stepping into another / self that exists in parallel', where 'when I travel back home, / I'm already there'. Miller urges us to scrutinise the past, reminding us that it is impossible to know

what to 'want more: certainty,/ or to finally set down this longing' for something that has always had no name.

Much delight from Miller's examination of forms of longing can be found throughout the collection. Particularly gorgeous coinages are scattered in the first third: a Cantonese song melts like a 'Cantopopsicle'; hunger 'telescopes' and fills strange distances; jellyfish 'moon-moons' swarm. In 'Social Distancing', touching is reinvented as 'transmutation' where 'you could touch anything you wanted and watch it change...A bench / became a hammerhead shark', which reminds us that all touch has always had a 'cost'. Later, 'Sonnet with Lighthouses', imagines the absurdity in the longing of a 'the ninth lighthouse' which has *'worse things happen at sea* cheerfully cross / stitched on a pillow it bought drunk off Etsy', and the longing of 'the fourteenth lighthouse' that 'hollers MARCO. / POLO, everyone you love shouts back'. The moreish quality of Miller's collection perhaps comes from the compact, concentrated ending of many of the poems, such as where in 'Sayang / Sayang', a careful mirroring makes 'such a shame to waste love / love, how much we've wasted' as bittersweet as it is melodic. Other endings are more aphoristic in nature – 'the collective noun for us [jellyfish] is an astonishment' stands up to much re-reading.

In a sequence in the middle of the collection, Miller describes jellyfish that 'are AM and FM radio waves, / passing each other in the same space, / unaware of each other's existence' and long for things just like 'people'. The suggestion, at the end of the sequence, in '[spineless menace]' that the jellyfish speaker can immigrate faster if they are 'willing to / be pulped for agricultural fertilizer' and have 'NO RECOURSE TO PUBLIC FUNDS stamped in squid ink on every tentacle' is both timely and a delight. Yet, there is a limit to how successful the idea of individual longing, as a vehicle for discussing contemporary politics, can be; the politics of migration is too expansive a subject to capture through a fairly narrow metaphor. In 'The Home Office' Miller asks us to decry a government that 'cheerfully mails you postcards that say 'wish you were here!'/ after deporting you'; this disrupts the momentum of the aquatic metaphors established earlier in the poem and somewhat distracts from the horror of a sea that is truly a pond 'choked...with scum' and patrolled with a belief that 'nobody necessarily stays anywhere forever'. I prefer the highly specific and subtle allusions to Chinese diaspora politics in 'Glitch Honorifics' where 'closeness to Chinese is through / the prism of mainland culture, / a standardized Beijing accent'; or, the intimacy of 'Persimmon abecedarian' where Miller asks us to 'imagine / jostling towards cold weather and unfamiliar countries / knowing it's the opposite direction of / every loved thing left behind' during a visit from the speaker's mother, where there is joy and delight in small, tender moments.

Poised for Prayer

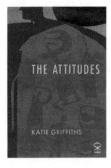

The Attitudes, Katie Griffiths (Nine Arches Press) £9.99
Reviewed by Jazmine Linklater

In Katie Griffiths' ambitious debut *The Attitudes* individual poems take on the weird, commonplace mixture of faith, flesh, life, doubt and death, while a number of longer sequences interweave throughout the collection. Griffiths' speakers assume various attitudes – physical and psychological – trying them on like outfits to compare in the dressing room mirror. It's a book made of things side-by-side, grappling with binaries to tease out their broader complexities. Under pressure are the mind and body; the tangible and metaphysical; real and illusive.

Many poems are written in two sections or short couplets. The title poem, for example, rewrites the biblical Beatitudes. Emulating those familiar couplets, Griffiths' version feels *more* mythical, populated by seemingly ancient and mysterious characters including 'earthmongers', 'soulscammers' and 'waterstabbers'. None here are blessed, and their various states are often the consequences of their own actions: 'Torrid are those who amass / for their trinkets will devour'. The poem operates as a sort of contents list, introducing characters who reappear later in the collection across a scattered sequence of expanded portraits. These poems oscillate through complex relationships. 'Moonbather', for example, 'wants to feel sorry for / you feeling sorry for her // and all the light you fail to exchange', but later, when she 'becomes moonlogged' grows 'innermost and full of retraction'. Griffith's strangely emphatic symbology is most arrestingly developed in 'Scargazer', where 'Scar' is 'suave as a flick, / clean as a plunge', evoking disturbing images of self-harm. But her rhythm and syntax beguile: 'see how easily / my arms went Scar / my back got Scar / my legs turned Scar'. This troubling mixture creates a conflicted kind of self-care or love, which stands in defiance against death:

> Can't you see
> the grace of Scar?
> Running a crack
> through the urn
> that wants your name.

The Attitudes scrutinises the messy doubts and desires that arise from an understanding of the body as the basis of Christian faith. Speakers often describe their experiences of detachment or distancing from their own bodies through the church, most explicitly in 'Dough must not enter the body', a sequence in six parts that portrays living with eating disorders. Here, 'the toilet bowl' is 'her white confessor' and the most 'holy work' is 'to dissolve. Disappear', as the body of Christ, as communion wafer, dissolves on the tongue. The ongoing incongruity of salvation and self-destruction is inescapable: 'Food is / life. / Food is / death'. The sequence is a stark presentation of how body dysmorphia keeps the mind and body apart, held in contention by a warped kind of faith: 'She holds her body to ransom. / Surely the negotiators will come'. This strained relationship between faith and agency permeates the collection, returning in poems on marriage, motherhood, and the deaths of loved ones, where incompatibilities deftly infer doubts and regrets.

Yet there is hope – most tangibly found in collective possibility. In 'Prayer Workshop', the group gives buoyancy to 'a prayer / shaped like a zeppelin that lurched uncertainly / until, willed upwards only by our gaze, / it bobbed and nudged the rafters'. A sense of human connectedness tempers the weight of more sombre subject matter, allowing a glimpse of the unfathomable magnitude that together we comprise. A number of poems attempt similar tempering through humorous word play, but it is sometimes unclear what these pieces achieve in the larger context of the collection, and jokes too often fall flat. 'Mes saints sans cafetières', for example, seems to have no bearing whatsoever on its title's sonic origins, Médecins sans Frontières (it really is a poem about saints not drinking coffee), and in 'Door, my tribe' the speaker's punning edges dangerously into dad joke territory: 'Did you know that / in the vestibule of door-makers / competition is unhinged?'. These, and a handful of occasional poems, interrupt the collection's more complicated interrogations.

His Vorpal Blade

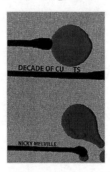

Decade of Cu ts, Nicky Melville (Blue Diode) £12
Reviewed by Greg Thomas

Nicky Melville's *Decade of Cu ts* is a collection of new and selected poems showcasing ten years of practice at the fringes of experimental poetics and agit-prop performance: a decade, too, of austerity-era conservative government (albeit recently mutated into a populist nostalgia cult) when cuts were the order of the day. The potty-mouthed pun – also published as a poem-badge – in Melville's title gets across something of both his animus and working method.

An obvious point of analogy for some of Melville's

poetry is that of his erstwhile mentor Tom Leonard, which found space on the page for forms of everyday language previously excluded from literature – indeed, whose quality of artistic and political legitimacy seemed somehow rooted in its defiant (and only apparent) non-literariness. Melville's 'heavy debate,' culled from conversations with a young offender during the poet's time working at HMYOI Polmont, even gestures towards the jazzily aestheticised demotics of Leonard's early verse: 'ma language is fucked up.' But it's notable that across this collection that form of phonetic exuberance is in relatively short supply.

Here's the distinction, perhaps: Leonard, at least in his early poetry, was known for committing to paper an approximation of language originating in an oral/aural domain: 'in the beginning was the sound.' Melville is more likely to start with the visual rather than sonic substance of language. His schooling in the concrete poetry movement of the 1960s is evident in a selection of 'thought experiments' – one or two-word poems with footnoted title – which adopt (and upturn) the visual logic of poster or billboard. 'WOR ', reads one piece (and, further down the page, 'in progress'). Another consists of the word 'scarcity' with two diagonal cut lines running through it; the appended title: 'austerity measures'. (This is poetry about poverty and despair, amongst other things.)

Another distinction, perhaps – staying on the question of cuts – is that Melville's is primarily a poetry of found and borrowed language, particularly that which assails us in an economy powered by the exchange of capital: in the beginning was the slogan. Sculpting an inert mass of advertising and propagandist babble, the poet unearths flashes of formal intrigue – 'Catch a great/cash ISA rate' ('bank poem') or bathos: 'Innocent / for kids // Reduced to clear' ('TESCO').

A set of long collage poems created by extracting sentences and phrases containing the word 'cut' from the major party manifestos for 2010, 2015, 2017 and 2019 gets close to the heart of the matter: '...We need / to cut /cuts and reorganisations / will be able to cut the cost / get a grip and cut / *that leads to violence. We will cu t/* police teams to cut crime...' ('2010 cu ts: Conservative.)' This is not a collage poetry of pure chance or surrealist flight of fancy, but neither is language rewired in the service of explicit polemic. The arrangement rather updates the aims of the cut-up method as formulated by Brion Gysin: to expose through rearrangement and repetition – a form of *ostranenie* – linguistic structures used insistently to mollify, confuse, and distract in the interests of power.

In spite of the moments of liberatory glee such a process can afford, Melville's is a poetic realm without much hope: 'life rips us to/pieces', he concludes in 'Sean-ec-doche,' dedicated to two recently deceased friends, including the poet Sean Bonney. If succour is to be found, it is in a number of more anecdotal, first-person sequences in which the lilt of lines down the page – very much in the Williams-Leonard trajectory – traces the rhythm of thought and speech in all its interpolated banality, paranoia, affection and intimacy. Here is the airport-lounge love poem 'Diversion Ends': 'in your text

/ you said / hey you / you didn't cry this time // I'm getting stronger / tho I already cried for you / when I was drunk / when I annoyed you.' Kitsch soap-opera cliché – 'I'm getting stronger' – here becomes a marker of genuine affection in a world where the means of expressing such sentiments has been lost in a fug of pop-culture sloganeering. Wordless bonds of friendship and love nonetheless subsist, we sense, beneath the surface of a compromised language. To paraphrase another 'thought experiment', our sentences still contain sentience.

I Say Heart

Naush Sabah, *Litanies* (Guillemot Press) £8
Suzannah V. Evans, *Brightwork* (Guillemot Press) £6
Diana Hendry, *Where I Was* (Mariscat Press, 2020) £6
Reviewed by Rory Waterman

I focus here on themed pamphlets. Each is very different but contains around twenty-five to thirty pages of poems: these are fairly sizeable publications, examples almost of a mid-length form between the book and what once would have been the 'standard' pamphlet, though of an increasingly common length for the medium. I do not favour absolutes, but too often, what might have been a successful themed pamphlet appears to have been bloated into a full-length collection with patently less successful poems, and increasingly I am convinced that around thirty pages is often the perfect length for such a volume. Here are three well-proportioned recent examples by way of testimony.

In 'Litany of Dissolution', on the first page of Naush Sabah's debut full-length pamphlet (following a 'double micro-pamphlet' published by Legitimate Snack in 2020), we read:

> time has folded up into me
>   I've been thrown by it
> like a child down a hill
>   standing up and brushing off grass
>   to find herself a woman

The poem is a slaloming stream of consciousness, one of several here but at four pages the longest of them, and displays many of Sabah's strengths: crystalline images and muscly enjambments, enriched by a mind at once subtle and forthright. At this point, though, you might be forgiven for thinking you've read it all before in a thousand self-indulgent poems. You haven't: 'now there's day after day after day / disappearing', she continues, 'and no god in them / to hook the carcass of any hope from', and the poem doesn't compromise in its depiction of what that means. 'Fiqh makes the munafiq' (glosses inform the uninitiated that this translates as 'Islamic law makes the hypocrite'), she writes in 'On Shahada' (translation: 'testimony (of faith)'):

I'm the hooded illusionist

and you a spectator watching me
fight against my own restraints.
Look. by this sleight of hand
I will make you believe I believe.

This gives a flavour of what the pamphlet puts at stake, and the certainty of its convictions. Certainty often makes poetry stale, but in this case it is the certainty of loss breeding passionately felt tensions. And passionately felt tensions can, in turn, breed self-indulgent sentimentality, but Sabah tempers them with impressive control, complexified through intertextual engagement with (or in some cases against) hadiths and Sufi songs. These poems marry their sometimes anguished conviction to an unusual panache for formal and linguistic dexterity. 'Of Monuments', a tiny poem of column-like single and double-line stanzas, comprises depictions of things presumed eternal, and ends: 'The deities have died but these columns endure.' 'Of Mercy', a two-stanza poem about an infant who might die, is one of the most affecting yet unaffected mirror poems I have read: 'if she lives / they'll praise God's mercy' and 'they'll praise God for his mercy / if she dies', each stanza either begins or ends, as 'my womb poor incubator still contracts'. The sonnet 'Of Myths and Messengers' turns every traditional element of the form – not least the expectation of unrequited love – on itself: 'The gods have needs and their messengers have pulpits: / someone must bleed, something must burn and smoke.' Who else is writing like this, now, and with at once such immediacy and breadth of reference? Sabah has a tendency sometimes to dilute by telling us what she has shown, but this is a stunning debut, that cliché for once fit for what it describes.

The pamphlet is sumptuously produced, as are all things from Guillemot Press. That includes Suzannah V. Evans's *Brightwork*, which is also obsessional, this time over the items clogging a boatyard. Evans wrote these poems while writer in residence at Underfall Yard in Bristol. (I had to venture to the Guillemot Press website to learn that: despite the press's attention to production values, it doesn't print pamphlets with blurbs – or page numbers, or contents pages – which is cute but also sometimes annoying.) Often, the poems are named for what they home in on: 'The Dredger Paddle', for instance, which – surprisingly, I'm sure you'll agree – is the subject of no other poem I can think of, and which 'is gently rusting, is gently resting by the powerhouse tower.' Or 'Buoy', a concrete poem shaped like its subject but with a revivifying metaphor worth waiting for (and not spoiling) at the end. The poems are often at first apparently wide-eyed in their middle-classness: these are things other people must use for often hard work, or so it seems from the poems, which can instead meditate on the items under examination. This is from 'Slipway', one of several prose poems:

I've seen you slide into the water, lowering yourself with an easy song, a sweet whining, a slow clanking; I've seen your wooden posts sink deeper like fins. There are other lovely things about you: your timber cradle, how you hold the hulls of boats so closely, how you keep your chocking stable, and whistle at the sight of a wooden deck. They call you a Heave-Up Slip, but the only heaving is done by the men around you, who lower poles, wind winches, puff and glance up at the sky.

'Lovely' it is, yes, but Evans often zooms out momently on the wider environment like this, so romanticisation is tempered by snatched insights into the lives of others, the lives that keep things here 'lovely' for the observer. As she writes in another poem,

I say *elbow*, and they think of the curved piece
of frame at the turn of the bilge, I say *heart*,
and they picture the centre of a section of timber.

Diana Hendry's new pamphlet is also obsessed with the finer details of a setting, in this case the house in which she grew up six and seven decades ago. The opening poem, 'Before Us', speaks of 'the grief that exuded from the walls like damp / which we couldn't get rid', the 'source' of which is 'the man who'd sold us the house', father to three boys 'All killed in the war. All.' That rather gives the sense that the home is doomed from the start, and the rest of the pamphlet goes about demonstrating ways in which it was. This is an extremely moving, unsentimental pamphlet tersely unfolding its unresolvable story, in which the past also belongs to the present, but only as something relived and unalterable. 'Mother! mother! / Let's get out of here', she writes, looking back, after a vivid depiction of 'woman's work' in a stifling mid-century, upper-middle-class household where the father hides 'behind his newspaper' dreaming of the sons he hasn't had and all is now over anyway.

Hendry does a superb job of throwing the most of us who haven't experienced it into the environment she describes. It's a bit like reading *Just William*, only with the japes and boys replaced by stoical sadness and girls, and possibility replaced by its vanquishment. In 'The Greenhouse', we learn that 'Before my father gave her away', the speaker's sister 'shut herself in there' with books and apples, as – in a perfect symbol of her predicament – 'terracotta pots of tomatoes' turned 'from green to red.' This isn't a pamphlet of lively experiments in form, but it is a meaningful tale of restriction, beautiful and pellucid in its unveiling.

Some Contributors

John Robert Lee is a Saint Lucian writer. His *Collected Poems 1975-2015* (2017) and *Pierrot* (2020) are published by Peepal Tree Press.

Charlotte Wetton's first pamphlet *I Refuse to Turn into a Hat-Stand* won the Michael Marks Awards 2017. She has published in Poetry Wales, Staple, Stand, and won a New Writing North award in 2019. She is studying for a PhD in Creative Writing at the University of Manchester. www.charlottewettonpoetry.wordpress.com @CharPoetry

N.S. Thompson is a poet, critic and translator and the non-fiction editor for Able Muse (USA). Two recent pamphlets are *After War* (New Walk Editions) and *Ghost Hands* (Melos Press).

Amy Acre is a poet from London, and the editor of Bad Betty Press. Her pamphlets *And They Are Covered in Gold Light* (Bad Betty, 2019) and *Where We're Going, We Don't Need Roads* (flipped eye, 2015) were each chosen as a Poetry Book Society Pamphlet Choice. Her debut collection is forthcoming in 2023.

Annie Fan recently graduated from Oxford, where she was president of the poetry society. Her first pamphlet, Wound-song, was published by Verve Press in May 2021 and her recent work appears in *The Offing* and *Puerto del Sol*, among others.

Jazmine Linklater is a poet and writer based in Manchester. Her most recent pamphlet, *Figure a Motion*, is published by Guillemot Press. She is one third of the No Matter collective and sits on the editorial board for Broken Sleep Books. She has worked at Carcanet Press since 2018.

Andrew Kahn teaches Russian literature at Oxford. His books include *Mandelstam's Worlds: Poetry, Politics, and Art in a Revolutionary Age*.

Helen Tookey lives in Liverpool. Her piece in this issue is part of a longer work in progress exploring her relationship with the work of Malcolm Lowry and Elizabeth Bishop.

Mark Dow is the author of *Plain Talk Rising* (poems) and *American Gulag: Inside U.S. Immigration Prisons* (California). His nonfiction manuscript *Each Thing Starts* was a 2021 semi-finalist for the *Seneca Review* Lyric Essay Book Prize, and his exploration of Beethoven's Opus 131 from that manuscript is in the Spring 2021 *Seneca Review*.

Judith Chernaik has written widely on Romantic poetry and music. Her most recent book is *Schumann: The Faces and the Masks* (Faber, 2018), now in paperback.

Sheri Benning's most recent collection of poetry is *Field Requiem* (Carcanet). Her previous collections include *The Season's Vagrant Light: New and Selected Poems* (Carcanet).

Kerrin P. Sharpe has published four collections of poetry (Victoria University Press). She has appeared in *Oxford Poets 13*, *Pedestal* and in *POETRY* (USA). In 2020 she was shortlisted for the Alpine Fellowship Writing Prize.

Jenny Lewis teaches poetry at Oxford University. Her recent publications include *Gilgamesh Retold* (Carcanet, 2018) and *Let Me Tell You What I Saw* (Seren, 2020), translations of Adnan Al-Sayegh's work.

Alastair Johnston is a partner in Poltroon Press of Berkeley, publishers of contemporary writing. His most recent book is *Dreaming on the Edge: Poets & Book Artists in California* (Oak Knoll Books).

Neil Davidson is a translator and newspaper columnist living in Chile, where he has published collections of columns and *El ceño radiante*, a biographical study of Gerard Manley Hopkins.

Andrew Hadfield is A Professor of English at the University of Sussex and a Fellow of the British Academy. His most recent book is *Literature and Class from the Peasants' Revolt to the French Revolution* (2021).

Vahni Capildeo is Writer in Residence at the University of York. Recent work includes *Like a Tree, Walking* (Carcanet, forthcoming), *The Dusty Angel* (Oystercatcher, forthcoming), and *Light Site* (Periplum, 2020).

Sophie Hannah is an internationally best-selling writer of psychological crime fiction, published in thirty-two languages and fifty-one territories. She has also published three novels featuring Agatha Christie's Hercule Poirot and five collections of poetry.

Sam Adams edited *Poetry Wales* in the 1970s and has been a contributor to *PNR* since 1982.

Rory Waterman is the author of three collections from Carcanet: the PBS Recommendation *Tonight the Summer's Over* (2013), shortlisted for the Seamus Heaney Award; *Sarajevo Roses* (2017), shortlisted for the Ledbury Forte Prize; and *Sweet Nothings* (2020).
Chris Miller is a widely published critic and translator. Co-founder of the Oxford Amnesty Lectures, he is the author of *Forms of Transcendence: The Art of Roger Wagner*.

Horatio Morpurgo is an environmental campaigner, essayist and poet. *Lady Chatterley's Defendant & Other Awkward Customers* was published by Just Press in 2011; *The Paradoxal Compass* by Notting Hill Editions in 2017.

Jonathan E. Hirschfeld, sculptor, divides his time between Paris, France and Venice, California. He has been deeply involved with portraiture for over forty years. He is also known for his work in bas-relief and photography.

Nicolas Tredell's most recent books are *Shakespeare: The Tragedies, Novels to Some Purpose* and a new edition of *Conversations with Critics* containing interviews originally published in *PNR*.

Rómulo Bustos Aguirre was born in 1954 near Cartagena de Indias, Colombia. He is a writer of slow poetry, inspired by the landscape and themes of his native Caribbean. A professor of literature at the University of Cartagena, he won the Blas de Otero Prize from the Universidad Complutense de Madrid in 2010 and was awarded Colombia's National Poetry Prize in 2019.

Colophon

Editors
Michael Schmidt
John McAuliffe

Editorial Manager
Andrew Latimer

Contributing Editors
Vahni Capildeo
Sasha Dugdale
Will Harris

Design
by Andrew Latimer

Editorial address
The Editors at the address on the right. Manuscripts cannot be returned unless accompanied by a stamped addressed envelope or international reply coupon.

Trade distributors
NBN International

Represented by
Compass IPS Ltd

Copyright
© 2022 Poetry Nation Review
All rights reserved
ISBN 978-1-8001-728-2-1
ISBN 0144-7076

Subscriptions—6 issues
 INDIVIDUAL–print and digital:
£39.50; abroad £49
 INSTITUTIONS–print only:
£76; abroad £90
 INSTITUTIONS–digital only:
from Exact Editions (https://shop.
exacteditions.com/gb/pn-review)
to: PN Review, Alliance House,
30 Cross Street, Manchester,
M2 7AQ, UK.

Supported by

Supported using public funding by
ARTS COUNCIL
ENGLAND